Early Advertising Alphabets, Initials and Typographic Ornaments

EDITED BY

Clarence P. Hornung

DOVER PUBLICATIONS, INC.

NEW YORK

Bibliographical Note

This fourth revised edition reprints the alphabets, decorative initials and typographic ornaments from *Handbook of Early Advertising Art: Mainly from American Sources/Typographical and Ornamental Volume/Third Edition,* as published in 1956 by Dover Publications, Inc. See "Preface to Fourth Revised Edition," opposite.

DOVER *Pictorial Archive* SERIES

This book belongs to the Dover Pictorial Archive Series. You may use the designs and illustrations for graphics and crafts applications, free and without special permission, provided that you include no more than ten in the same publication or project. (For permission for additional use, please write to: Permissions Department, Dover Publications, Inc., 31 East 2nd Street, Mineola, N.Y. 11501

However, republication or reproduction of any illustration by any other graphic service, whether it be in a book or in any other design resource, is strictly prohibited.

Library of Congress Cataloging-in-Publication Data

Handbook of early advertising art. Selections.
    Early advertising alphabets, initials, and typographic ornaments / edited by Clarence P. Hornung. — 4th rev. ed.
        p.   cm. — (Dover pictorial archive series)
    Abridged ed. of: Handbook of early advertising art. 3rd ed. 1956.
    Includes bibliographical references.
    ISBN 0–486–28405–0 (pbk.)
    1. Alphabets.   2. Initials.   3. Printers' ornaments.   4. Decoration and ornament—History—19th century.   5. Commercial art. I. Hornung, Clarence P.   II. Title.   III. Series.
NK3630.H36   1995
686.2′24—dc20   94-24465
                                                                                CIP

Manufactured in the United States of America
Dover Publications, Inc., 31 East 2nd Street, Mineola, N.Y. 11501

PREFACE
TO FOURTH REVISED EDITION

Appearing in paperbound form for the first time, this work, formerly the "Typographical and Ornamental Volume" of HANDBOOK OF EARLY ADVERTISING ART, omits the chapters on type faces but retains the alphabets, decorative initials and ornaments introduced in the third edition in their entirety. The plates have been repaginated, minor corrections made to the captions, and plates referred to in the Bibliography have been renumbered.

1995   The Publisher

PREFACE
TO THIRD REVISED EDITION

Users of the first and second editions of this work, formerly titled EARLY AMERICAN ADVERTISING ART, have indicated a want for more specimens of decorative initials and for full alphabets. The book has accordingly been enlarged by the addition of fifty-two plates of ornamental alphabets and ten plates of borders. The selection and arrangement of the new material was made by Alexander Nesbitt, author of LETTERING and member of the faculties of New York University and of Cooper Union.

It was found that while early American advertising used decorative letters profusely, few of them were designed in America; they were mostly copied from European designs. In order to provide a representative assortment of such letters and alphabets, it was necessary to draw upon European sources as well as American. The qualification AMERICAN was accordingly dropped from the title of this book, but the great bulk of the contents remains American in design and spirit.

The historical development of the decorative initial is a fascinating study, a little knowledge of which can be most illuminating to the typographical craftsman. Mr. Nesbitt has sketched this development in a preface to the section on Alphabets and Decorative Initials and in notes on the plates.

All of the new plates in this third edition were photographed directly from the original sources—type specimen books of the 19th century and earlier.

1956   The Publisher

PREFACE TO
SECOND REVISED EDITION

The typographical and ornamental material in this volume is a tenfold expansion over the material that appeared in the first edition. All the material has been rephotographed in order to achieve greater clarity. The section containing type specimens has been greatly expanded and reorganized. New sections on borders, signboards, scrolls, rules and panels, ornaments, and ribbons have been added.

The following specimen catalogues were the main sources for this collection: MacKellar, Smiths and Jordan; *New York Type Foundry Specimen of Printing Types Cast* by John T. White; James Conner's Sons; Blomgren and Co. Some material also came from *Ames Guide to Self Instruction in Practical and Artistic Penmanship* and *Real Pen Work Self-Instructor in Penmanship* published by Knowles and Maxim.

The publisher is deeply indebted to S. Guy Oring for his assistance in preparing this volume.

1953   The Publisher

CONTENTS

THE PLATES

The illustrations shown on the following plates have been taken, for the most part, from type specimen books representative of the nineteenth century. A careful inspection of these volumes reveals that the cuts not only appear repeatedly in subsequent issues, but in the pages of several different foundries as well. A listing of these source books will be found in the Bibliography, together with notes on the plates.

PREFACE TO ALPHABETS AND DECORATIVE INITIALS

All of us have some interest in decorative initials. We remember them from the fabulous books of our childhood, or we have seen them in the present-day books that we give to our own children. They come to us, really, out of the ancient days of legend and fable. Much of the charm, the fascination, of the medieval book lies in the use of initials to ornament and emphasize the text; and it is mostly from this period of book production that all later artists, type-designers and letter-designers have derived their inspiration for ornamental letters.

It was just at the end of the Middle Ages that the printing art came into startling and sudden importance as a producer of books. The manuscript writers, illuminators, and rubricators were faced with a competition that they were unable to overcome. For some time manuscripts and printed books were produced side by side. Of course, the printed book had to resemble the manuscript in most respects; and the student of early books knows this well. One of the concessions that many of the first printers made was to allow areas for the insertion of initials and illumination, which were to be put into the book by hand. It is clear that decorative initial usage followed an unbroken tradition from the manuscript book over into the first output of the printing-press. This is the point to be noted in even the slightest study of initial letters.

As the printer took over more and more of book production, it must have seemed foolish to him not to print the initials too. He therefore began to devise initials, cut in wood or type metal, which could be printed along with the text or stamped in separately in other colors. These ornamented letters, within the limitations imposed by the typographic process, were exactly what the Gothic initial artist had been drawing or painting into books for many generations. The lily-of-the-valley initials of Günther Zainer, which start the special collection of ornamental alphabets in this book, illustrate the derivation very well. They are fairly close to being the first set of decorative, typographic initials; they have been copied and "swiped" right up to the present day; and they may well serve us as a springboard from which to take off on this investigation of ornamented initials.

The other powerful stream of influence that affected all ornament and decoration was the Renaissance. The German printers who went into the Italian area to start presses there soon found that they had to produce type and initials to follow the style of the humanist manuscript. Printers such as Ratdolt, therefore, designed initials with a somewhat different flavor. The example of his initials shows a design which, again, has been copied over and over. It is not altogether by accident that Ratdolt is called the father of decorative typographic initials.

A third kind of initial was the illustrated or historiated letter. This style is very well shown in the examples of woodcut alphabets in our selection. It is amazing how much could be pictured in these little backgrounds for initial letters. Even great artists like Holbein and Dürer found in such a series of initials a most interesting and challenging project.

To skip lightly over history and influence is the final task of this introduction. The continuation of the Renaissance and the center of fine book production was situated in the French area during the first half of the 16th century. Sets of initials by Geoffroy Tory and other designers again set up an influence that has lasted into modern times, in the work of Frederic Goudy, Bruce Rogers, and others. The Low Countries took precedence in book and typographic production during the 17th century; and the tradition of decorative letters was continued, along with the introduction of engraved initials. Each area of western Europe, in its own time, produced series of decorative alphabets with which to ornament and enliven the typographic page.

Craftsmanship declined over the centuries. The 18th-century English book was nothing to brag about until John Baskerville displayed his examples of clean, chaste book production. But he left out all initials that could be called decorative. Here was started the movement against the use of the ornamented initial in books—at least against the traditional decorated letter.

With the development of lithography in the 19th century the type foundries were faced with a great competitor—for the lithographer could draw any and all sorts of letters on his stone; his imagination was free to roam, and it did. The type foundries took up the challenge, however, and produced during the 19th century a volume of ornamented types and alphabets that might be said to stagger the imagination. Fantastic is a mild word for many of these creations. In the latter part of this section devoted to initials, there have been included enough specimens to show the range of the 19th-century typographic fancy. These are the "Victorian," "Americana," etc.—ornamented types that went into the books and advertising that our grandfathers and great-grandfathers looked at.

It is hoped that in this addition to the history of early advertising typography the student or designer will find an exposition of that most important factor, the ornamented initial. What he must recall in looking at the 19th-century productions is that they were designed under the two main revival influences of the period: the Gothic and Renaissance revivals, especially in England. Any brief perusal of the examples shown will confirm this view. As for the fantastic, almost surrealistic, typographic concoctions of this whole era, one must regard them as the products of certain whimsical, sentimental, and sometimes psychotic elements in the then-prevailing European character. We in America were a part of this chain of typographic development. We imported type and type-designers to develop our own industry and service our budding advertising business.

1956   Alexander Nesbitt

The famous lily-of-the-valley alphabet used by Günther Zainer
at Augsburg, about 1475

Some of Erhard Ratdolt initials, showing use of italianate ornament,
1476-1486

The printing center of Lyons used initials like these—first quarter
of the 16th century

A simple and charming set of Venetian initials—Philippus Pincius, 1504

The early German printers in Spain used initials such as these, 1492-1497

Initials in criblé manner, possibly cut in metal—André Bocard, Paris, 1491-1531

A kind of initial often used in the late 15th century—these at Lyons

Initials from the Ferrara-Florence area, apparently used by various printers, 1497

Birds, beasts, and flowers—used by Jacques Sacon, Lyons, 1519

Jacob Köbel's initials, 1518—Italian influence on German printers

Cherubs and children by Anton Woensam, used at Cologne, first half of the 16th century

The female form and the vagaries of love—from the Egenolff press, Frankfurt, 1543

Geoffroy Tory's fame rests largely on these lovely initials—Paris, 1522-1529

Oronce Finé, the mathematician, designed these initials in Paris, 1532

A set of thistle initials used by the printer Denys Janot, 1544

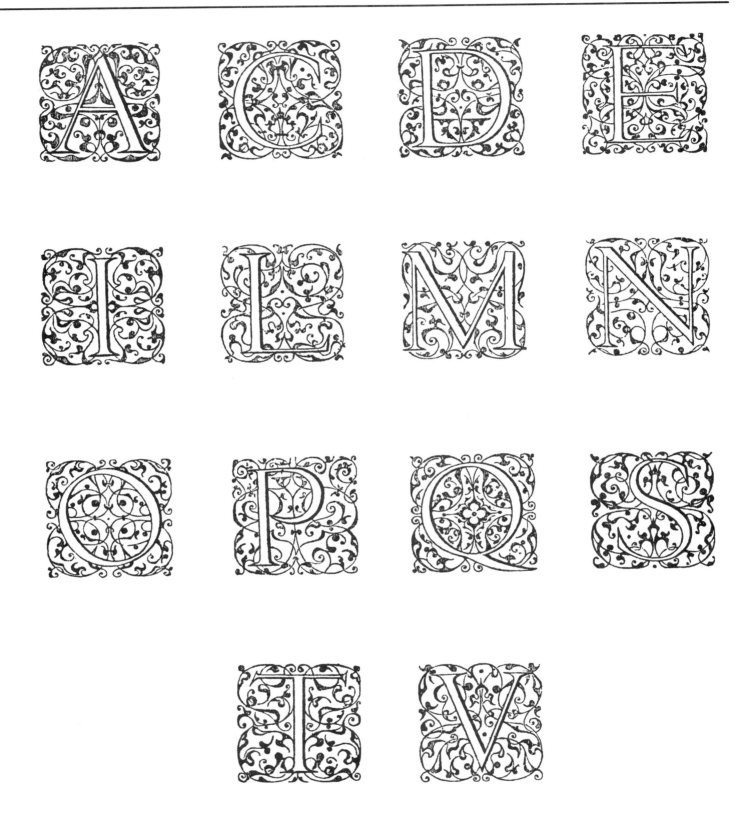

Arabesques like these were popular after 1550—used by
Jean Crespin at Geneva

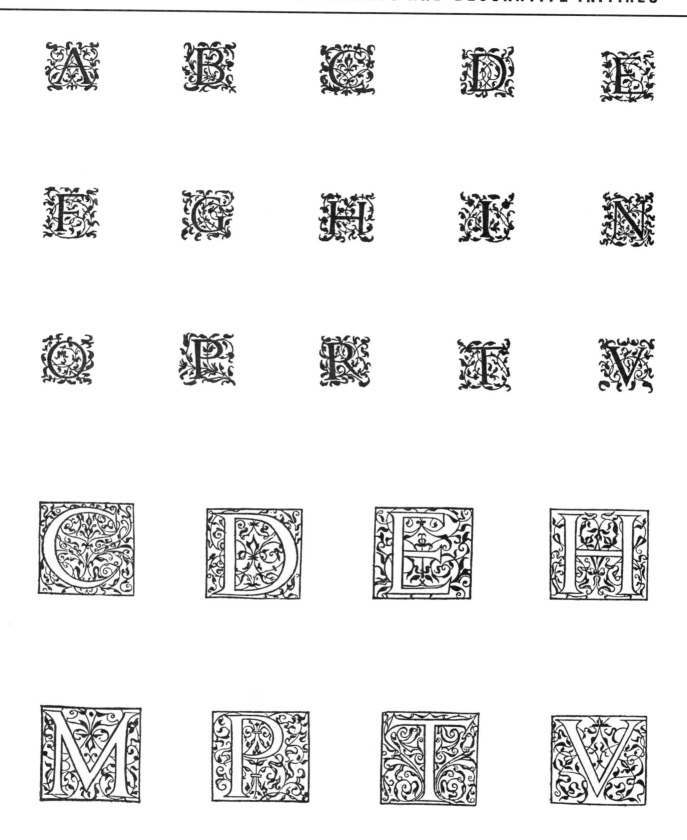

Two sets of French initials in the arabesque manner—
later part of the 16th century

These initials are related to those used by Plantin and by Adam Berg

This sort of initial was used in music books about 1600

Dutch initials of the 17th century—the basket-of-flowers was a
much-used design

The blocks of these 17th-century initials still exist at the firm of
Enschedé, Haarlem

Initials were also produced by copperplate engraving—these are Dutch, late 1600's

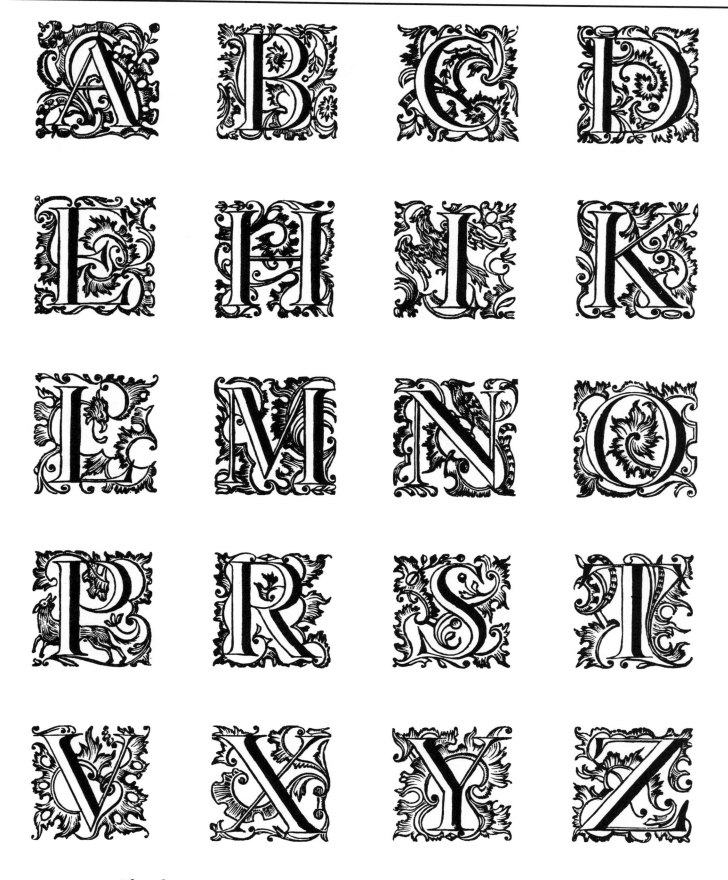

These letters were cut on metal by J. F. Rosart—bought by Enschedé in 1760

Woodcut initials by Jean Michel Papillon—first shown in Paris, 1760

Jean Michel was a son of Jean Papillon, the famous manufacturer
of fine wallpapers

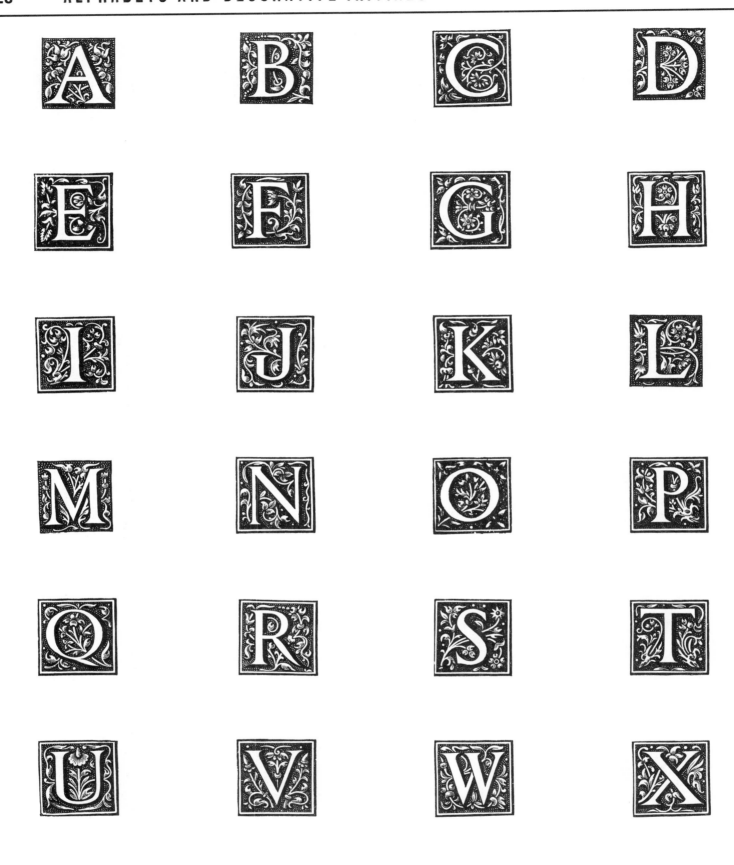

A revival design—used by the Chiswick Press in England,
middle of the 19th century

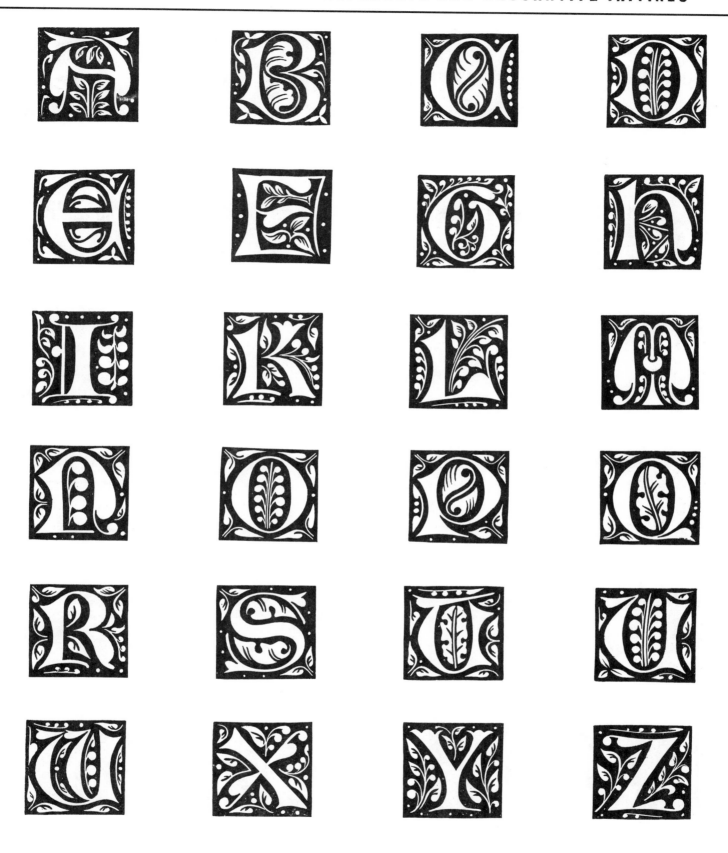

A rather original alphabet used by the Chiswick Press—
based on Gothic initials

A set of initials used in England about 1880—possibly of
French origin, cut in wood

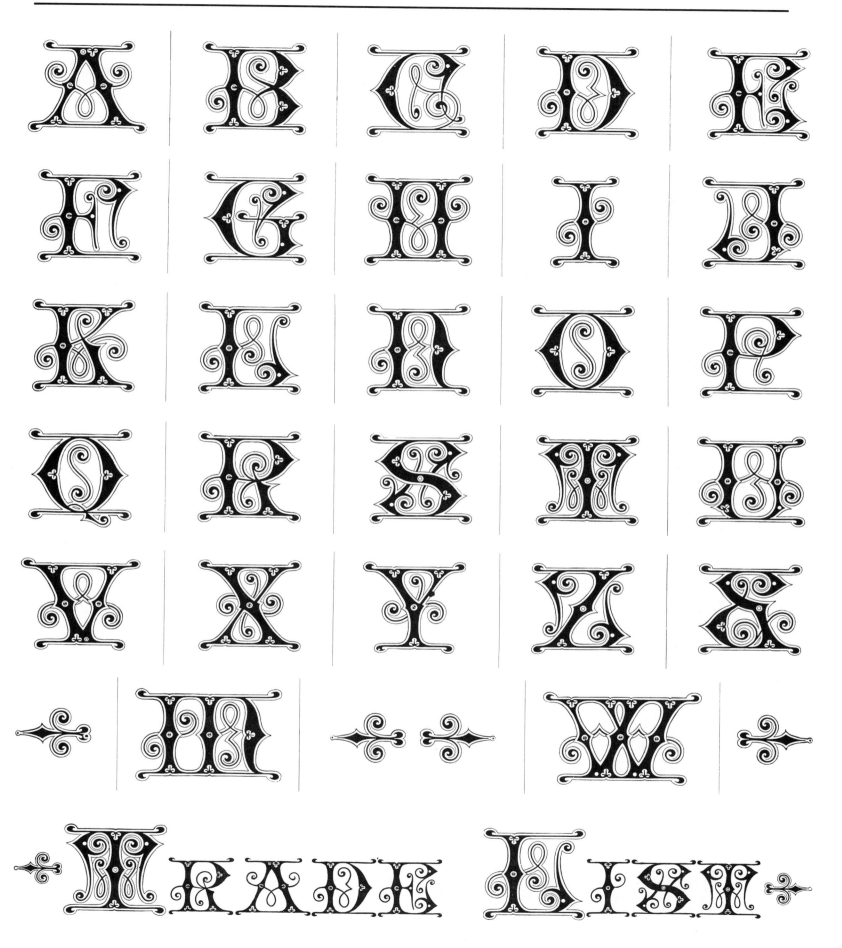

These initials were called Medieval, but they are really Victorian gingerbread, 1890

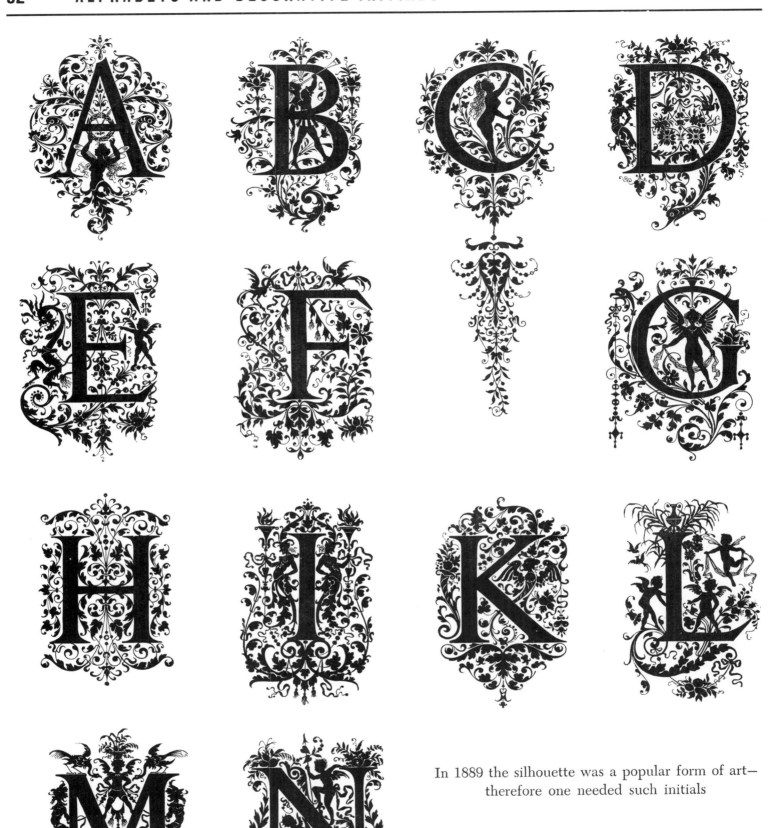

In 1889 the silhouette was a popular form of art—
therefore one needed such initials

More silhouette initials—they are essentially a variety of the arabesque

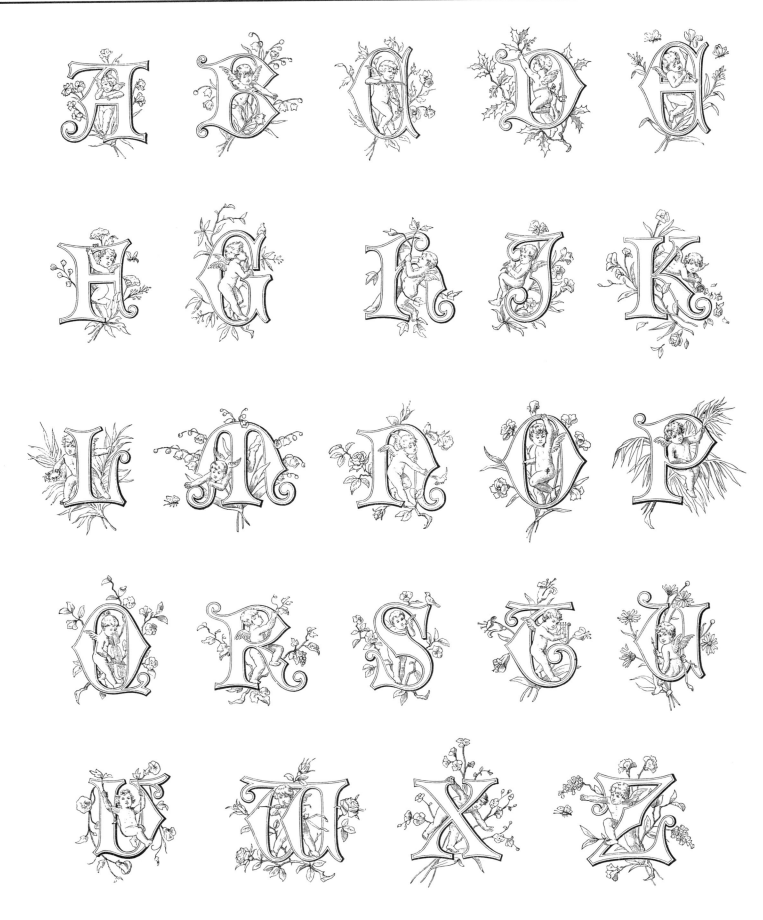

Gothic initials with superimposed sentimentality—called Amorette,
and used about 1889

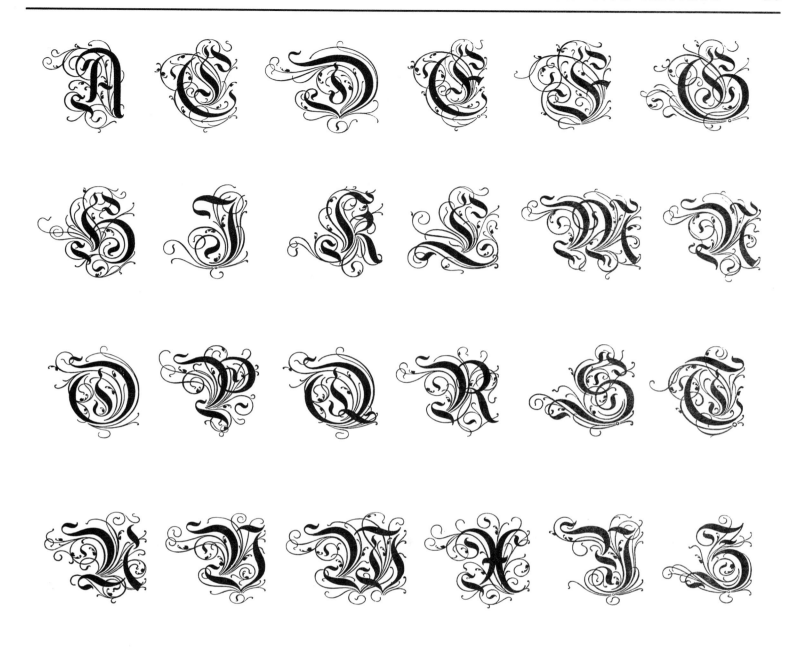

Revival of a Gothic chancery letter—related to the Fraktur design—
German 1880's

TUSCAN.

ABCDEFGHIJKLMN
OPQRSTUVWXYZ &

abcdefghijklmnopqr

12345 stuvwxyz 67890.

F. S. Copley. Del.

ITALIAN PRINT

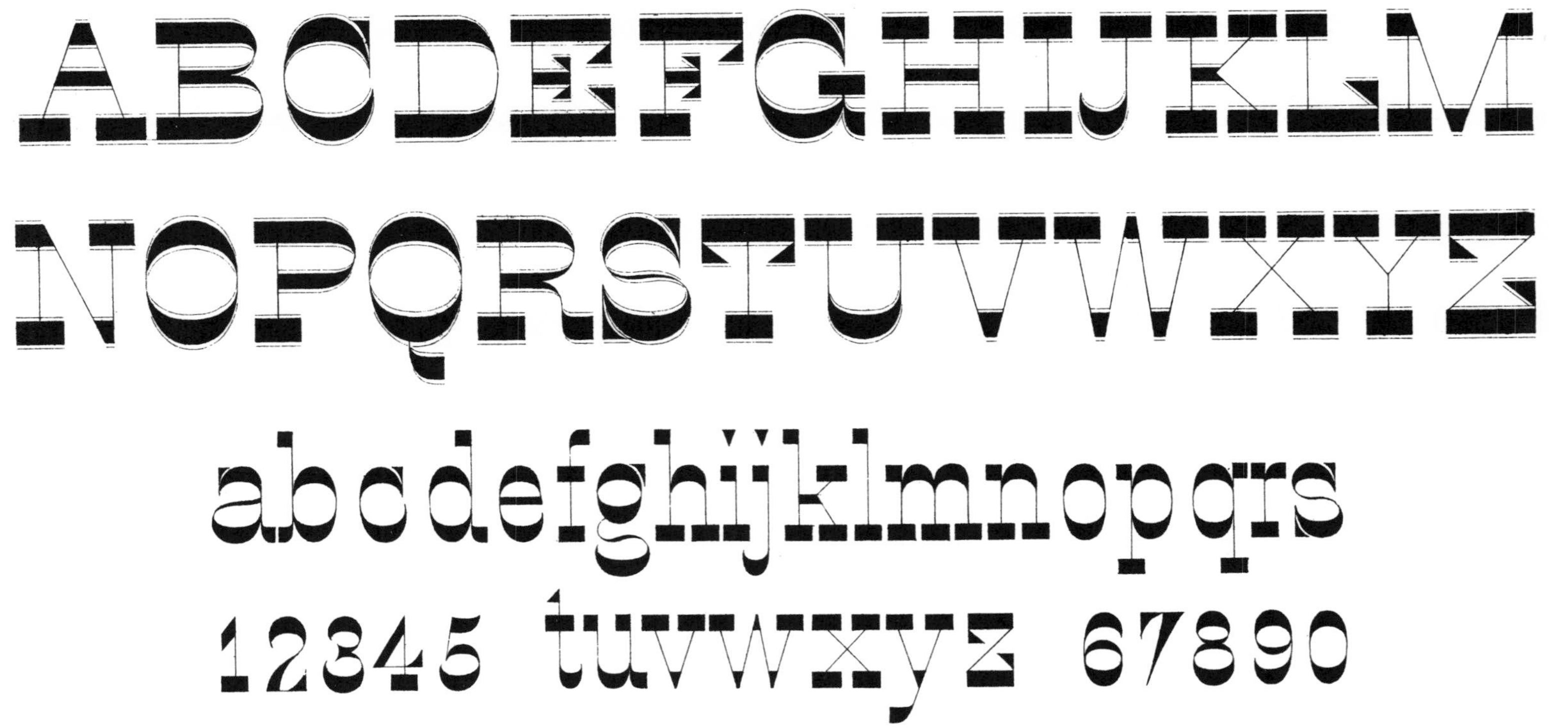

ABCDEFGHIJKLM

NOPQRSTUVWXYZ

abcdefghijklmnopqrs

12345 tuvwxyz 67890

Two basic 19th-century styles—Tuscan, with forked ends, and Italian

ROMAN PRINT, VARIOUSLY SHADED.

ABCDEFGHI
JKLMNOPQR
STUVWXYZ&

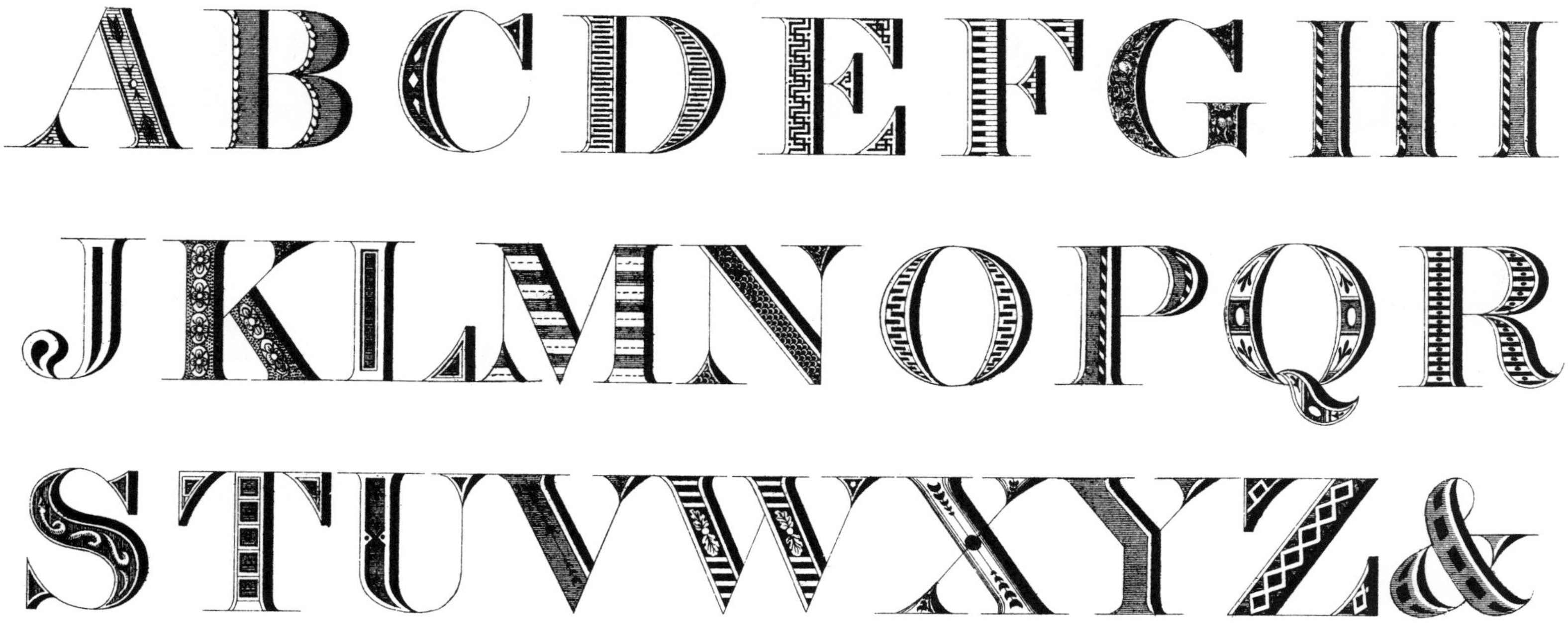

ITALIC PRINT, VARIOUSLY SHADED.

ABCDEFGHIJKLM

NOPQRSTUVWXYZ

abcdefghijklmnopqrstuvwxyz.

Here are a few of the shading ideas used by 19th-century lithographers and engravers

Gothic revival of the 1880's, with non-Gothic doodling as a
background—German

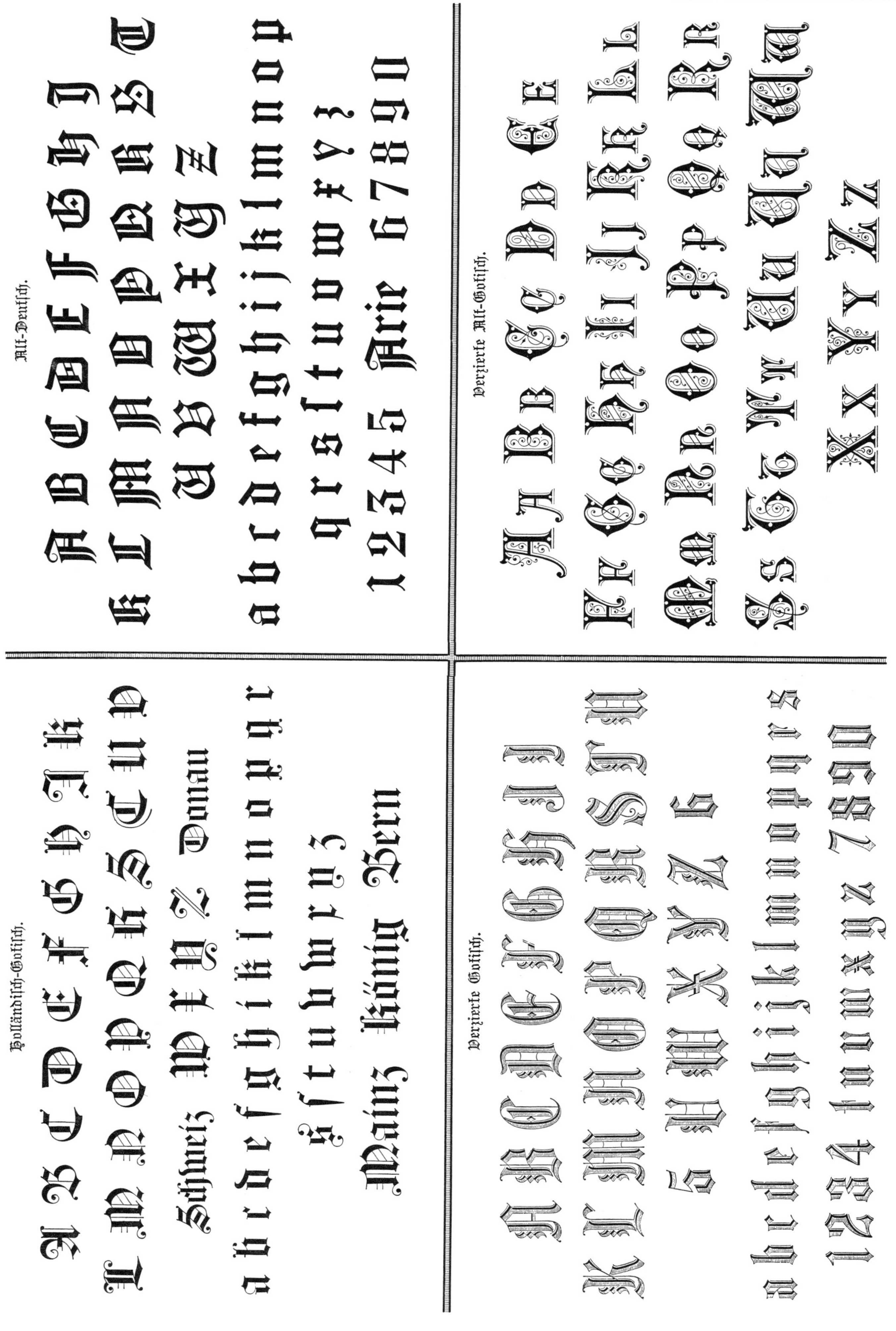

Alt-Deutſch.

ABCDEFGHIJ
KLMNOPQRST
UVWXYZ
abcdefghijklmnop
qrsſtuvwxyz?
12345 Arie 67890

Verzierte Alt-Gotiſch.

Holländiſch-Gotiſch.

ABCDEFGHIJK
LMNOPQRSTUV
WXYZ Donau Schweiz
abcdefghijklmnopqr
ſtuvwxyz
Mainz König Bern

Verzierte Gotiſch.

Nineteenth-century varieties of Dutch, German, and decorated Gothics

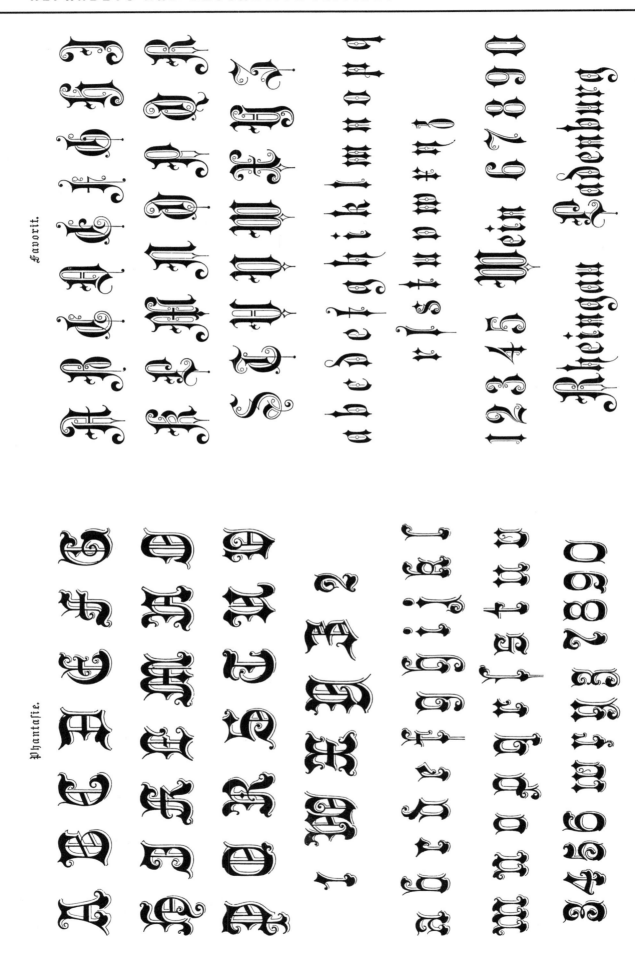

Here are two Gothic alphabets with typical 19th-century
aberrations and trimmings

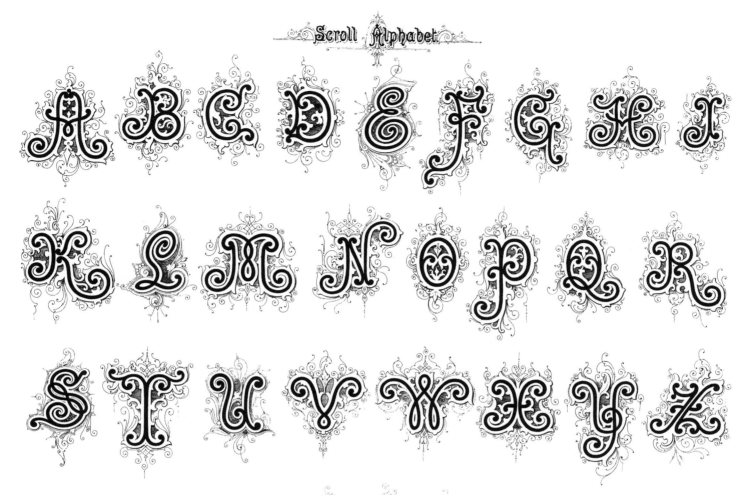

Scroll Alphabet

Rustic Alphabet

Shrubbery of all kinds was used for initials during the last part of the 19th century

ROMAINE MIDOLLINE.

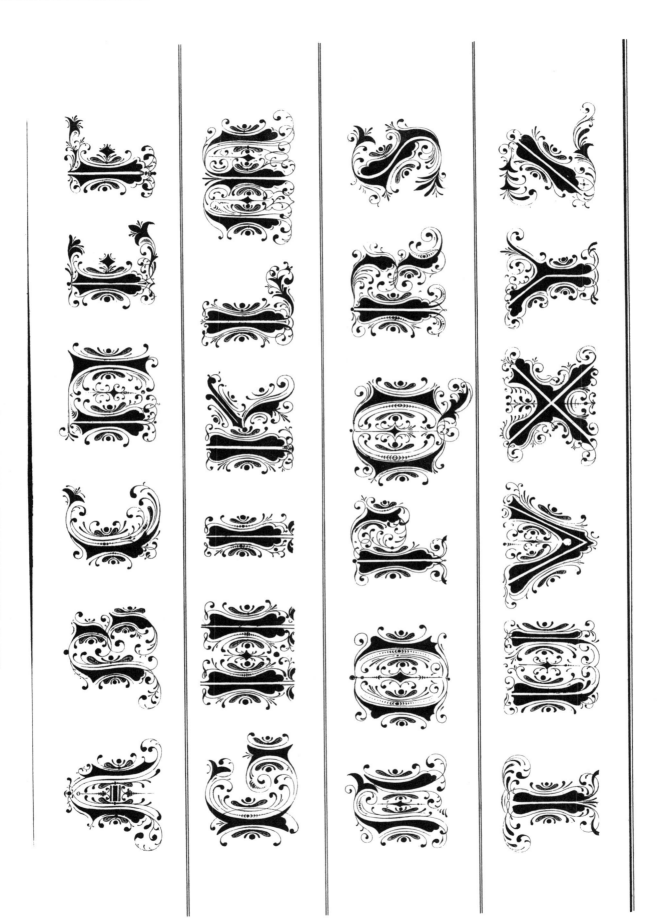

A 19th-century alphabet derived from an Italian 16th-century style

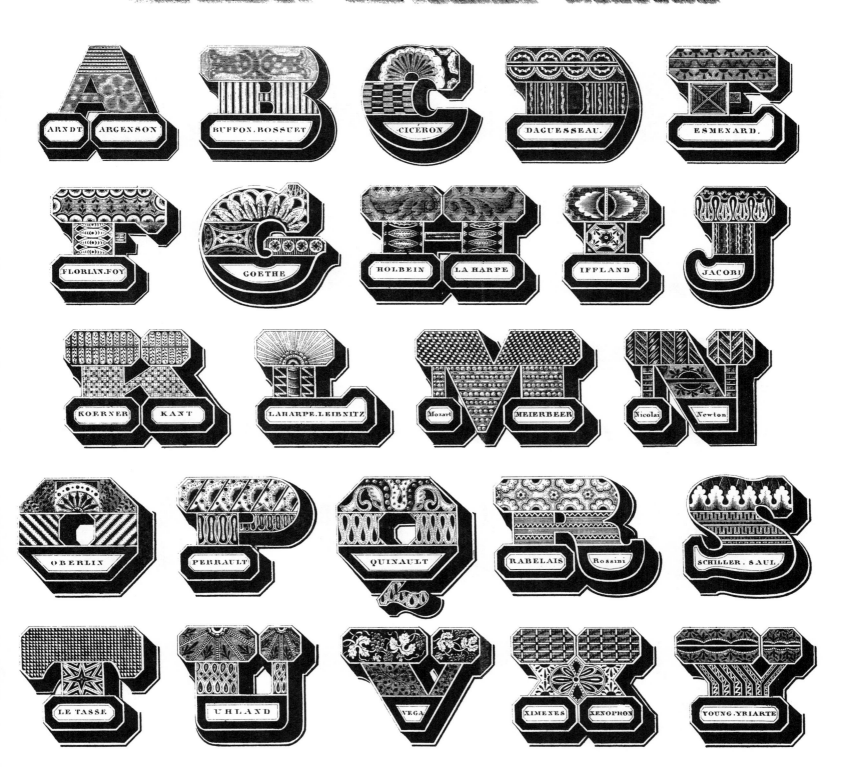

This 19th-century alphabet was called Lapidaire Monstre—
which it is, to say the least

Rather fine late 19th-century revival of Florentine Renaissance
initials—German

Second half of the Florentine alphabet—color and texture are uneven
(note the S)

Schmale Jonisch.

ABCDEF
GHIJKLMN
OPQRSTUV
WXYZ

Schattierte Jonisch.

ABCDEFGHI
JKLMNOPQRST
UVWXYZ
abcdefghijklmno
pqrstuvwxyz
1234567890

Halbfette Egyptienne.

ABCDEFGHIJ
KLMNOPQRSTU
VWXYZ
abcdefghijklmno
pqrstuvwxyz

Breite Egyptienne.

ABCDEFGHIJKLMNO
PQRSTUVWXYZ
abcdefghijklmnopqrstu
1234567890

Lichte Jonisch.

ABCDE
FGHIJK
LMNOP
QRSTUV
WXYZ

Kursiv.

ABCDEFGHI
JKLMNOPQRS
TUVWXYZ
abcdefghijklmn
opqrstuvwxyz
1234567890

Another basic 19th-century style: Egyptian, sometimes Ionic, better called Square Serif

Clarendon.

A B C D E F G H I J K L M N O P Q R S
T U V W X Y Z 1 2 3 4 5 6 7 8 9 0
a b c d e f g h i j k l m n o p q r s t u v w x y z

Richard BREMEN Wagner

Schriftgiesserei von Bauer & Comp. in Stuttgart.

Breite verzierte Clarendon.

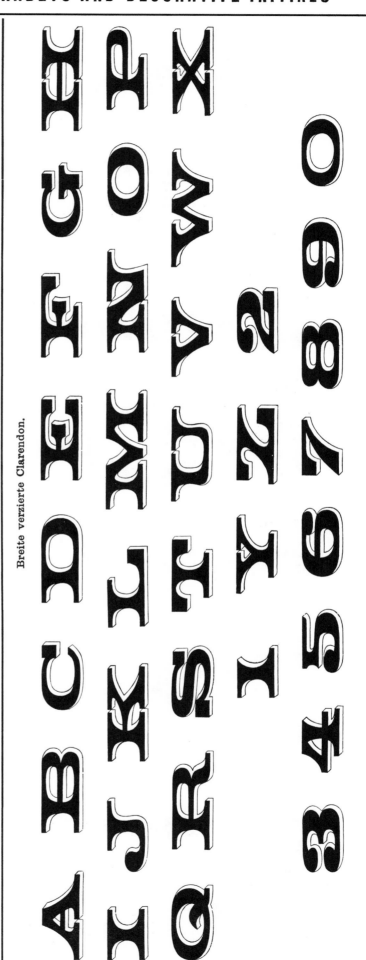

The Clarendons were also developed in the 19th century—also a basic style

Breite (geschweifte) Italienne.

ABCDEFGHIJ
KLMNOPQRST
UVWXYZ
123456
7890

Schriftgiesserei von Genzsch & Heyse in Hamburg.

Italienne Kursiv (verziert).

A B C D E F G H I J
K L M N O P Q R S T
U V W X Y Z
a b c d e f g h i j k l m n o p
q r s t u v w x y z
1 2 3 4 5 6 7 8 9 0

Schriftgiesserei von Schelter & Giesecke in Leipzig.

Italienne.

ABCDEFG
HIJKL
MNOPQRS
TUVW
XYZ
123456
7890

Schriftgiesserei von Genzsch & Heyse in Hamburg.

Italienne Kursiv.

A B C D E F G H
I J K L M N O P Q R
S T U V W X Y Z

Schriftgiesserei von Julius Klinkhardt in Leipzig.

Schattierte Italienne.

ABCDEFGHIJKL
MNOPQRSTUVW
XYZ ghijkl
abcdef
mnopqrstuvwxyz

Schriftgiesserei Flinsch in Frankfurt a. M.

Breite Italienne.

ABCDEFGHIJKLMN
OPQRSTUVWXYZ
abcdefghijklmnopqrstu
vwxyz 1234567890

Italian is distinguished by wrong-way weights—there is little reason
for the name

These initials cost 60¢ apiece in 1890—with special filigree border $1.00

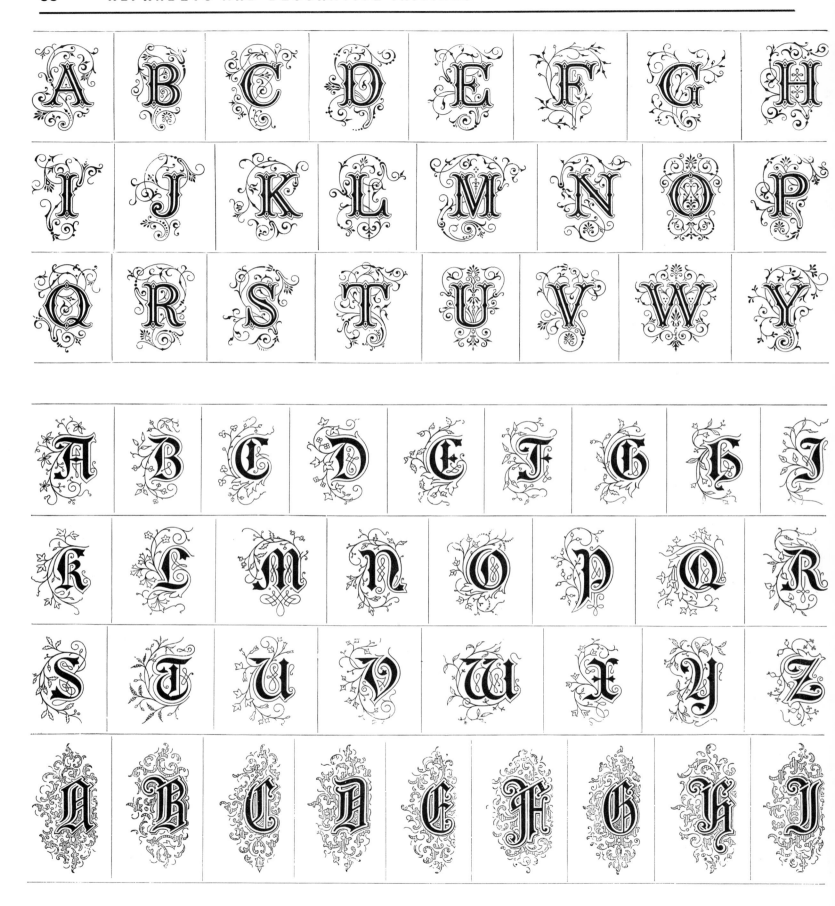

Arabesque designs appeared again in the 19th century—
some were rather pretty

Gothic-revival initials based on the 14th-century "closed letter"
design—1890

English revival of the arabesque design dating from about 1900

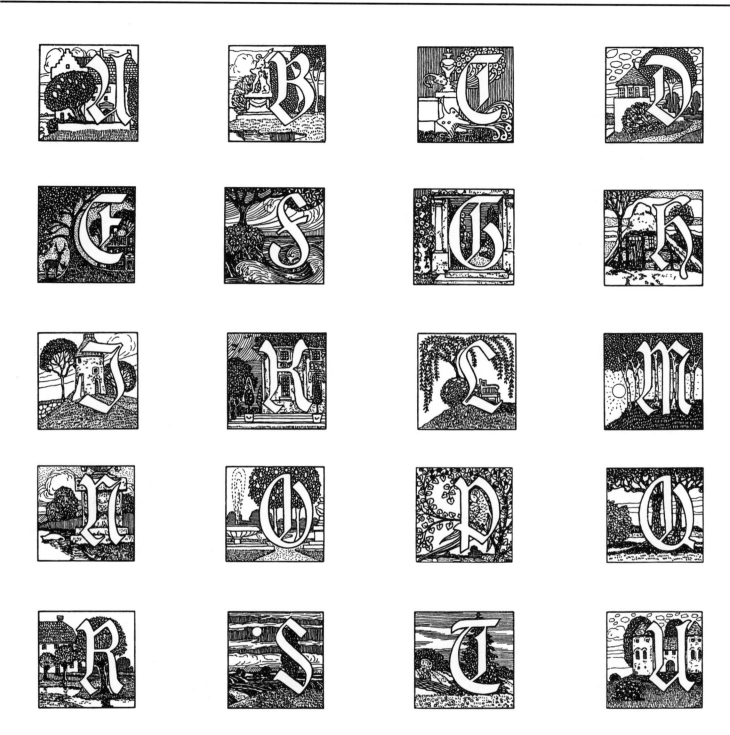

A Jugendstil alphabet produced in Germany in the early 1900's

A set of wood-engraved initials—the terrors of night life—
Riga, Latvia, 1924

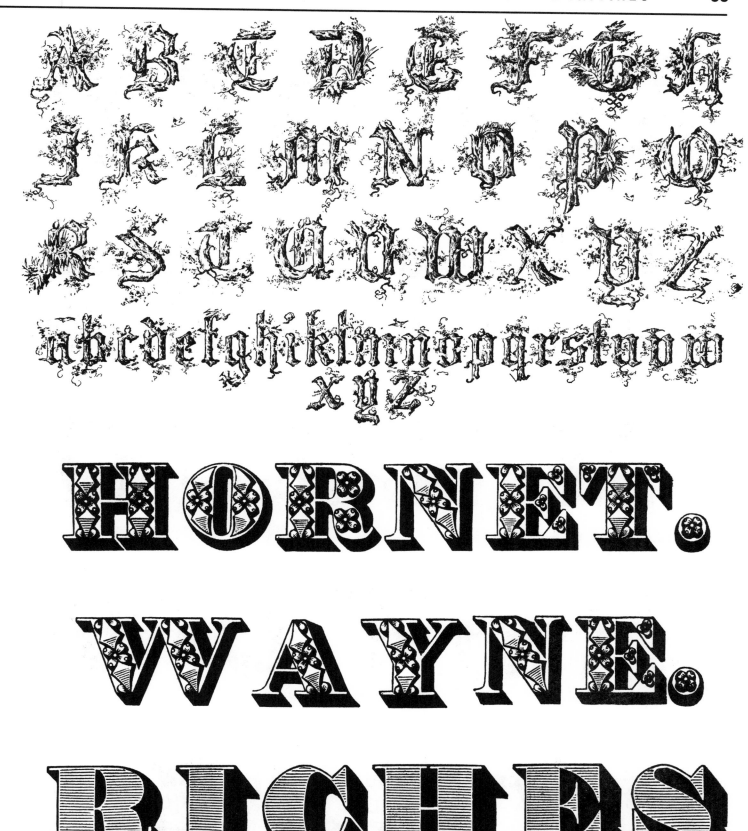

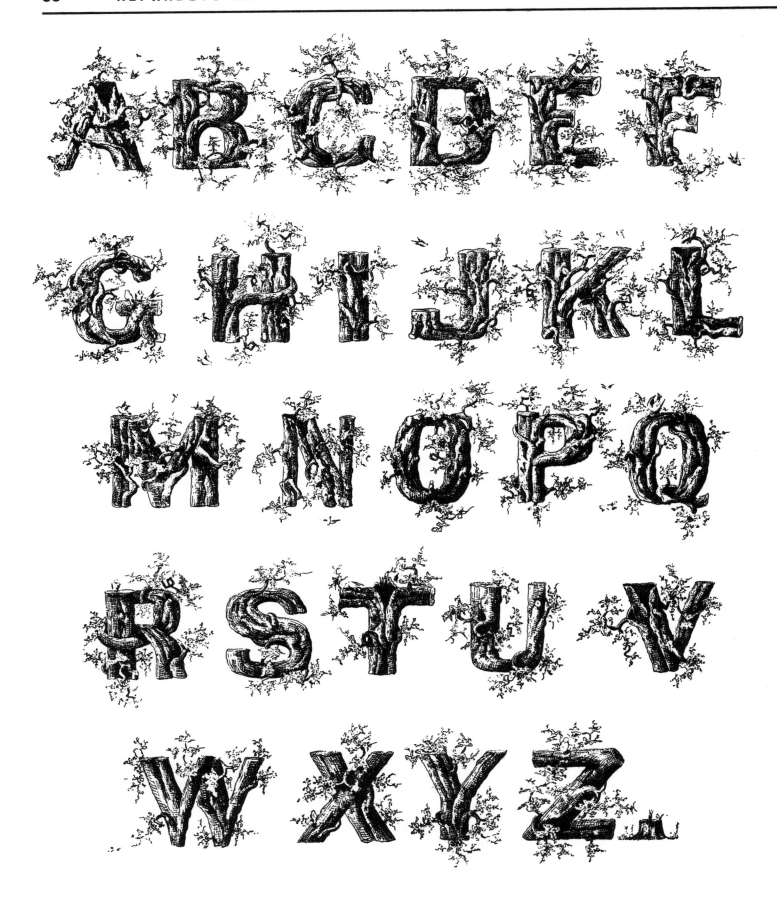

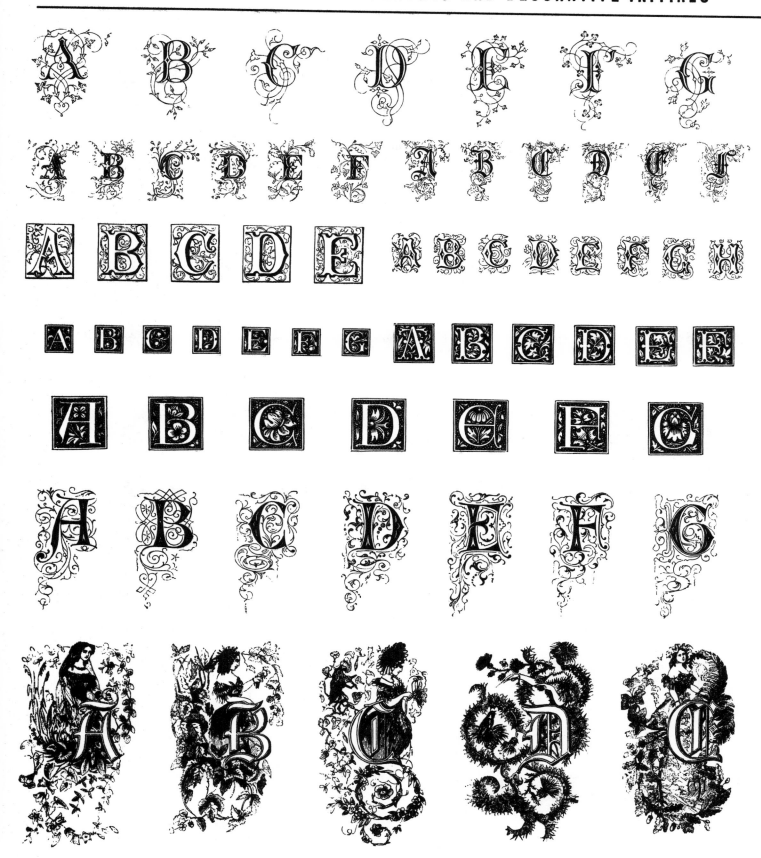

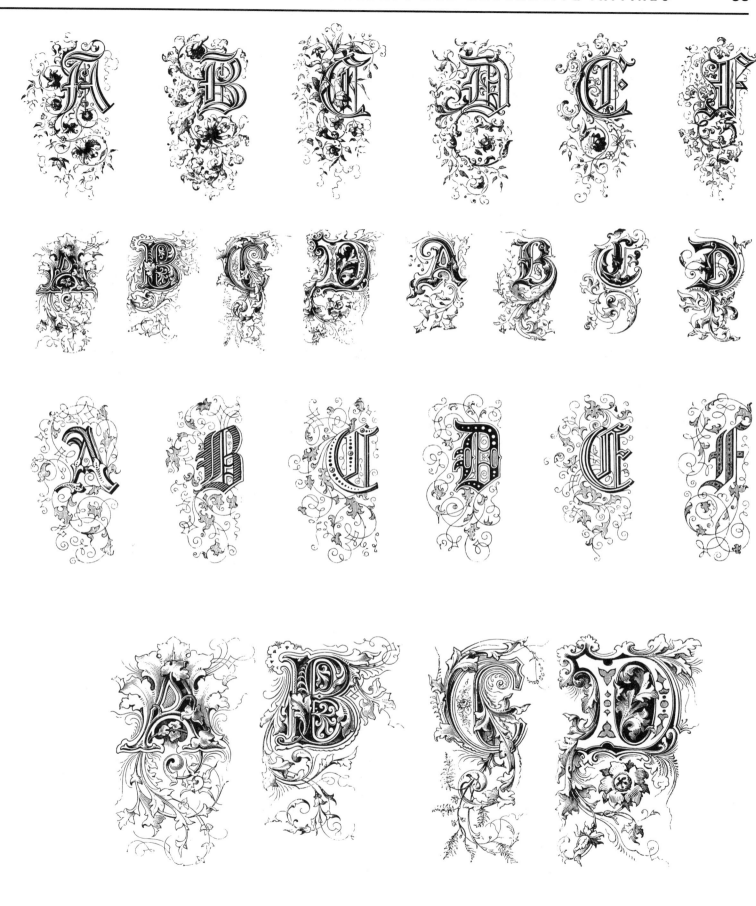

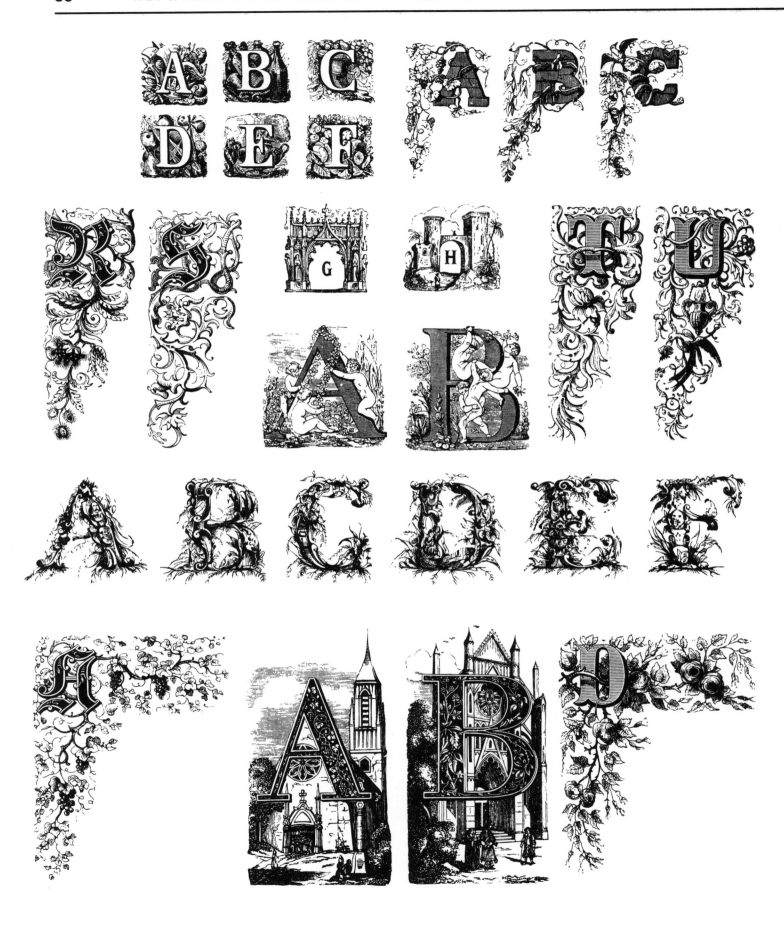

WE POINT with pride to the productions of the
BRAINCRAFT AND HANDICRAFT
of those connected with this establishment
during the century which is now approaching its close

BILLHEAD LOGOTYPES.

Ornamental Flourishes.

ORNAMENTAL FLOURISHES.

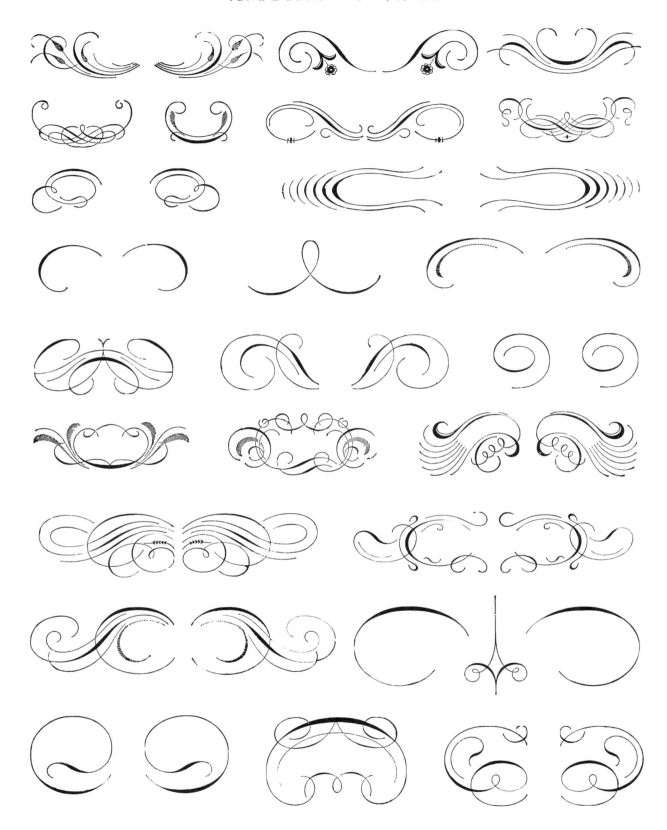

ORNAMENTAL FLOURISHES.

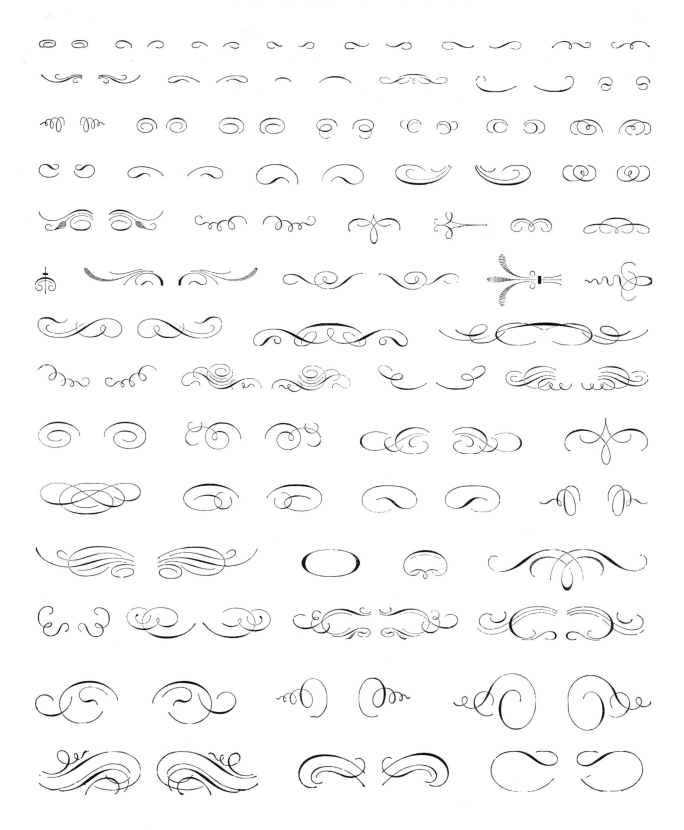

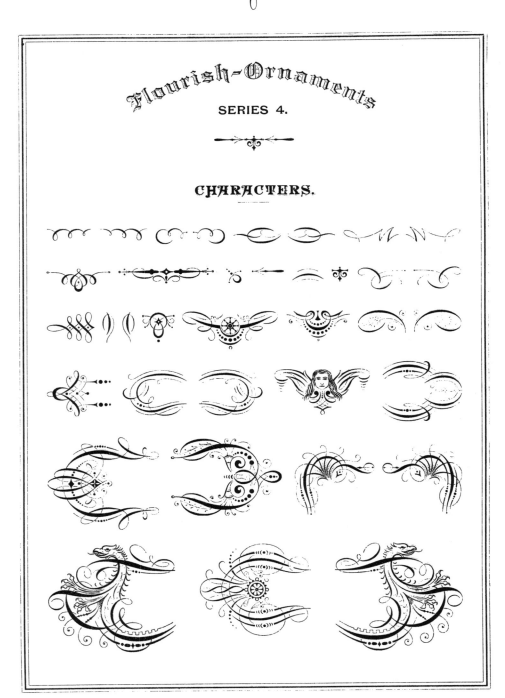

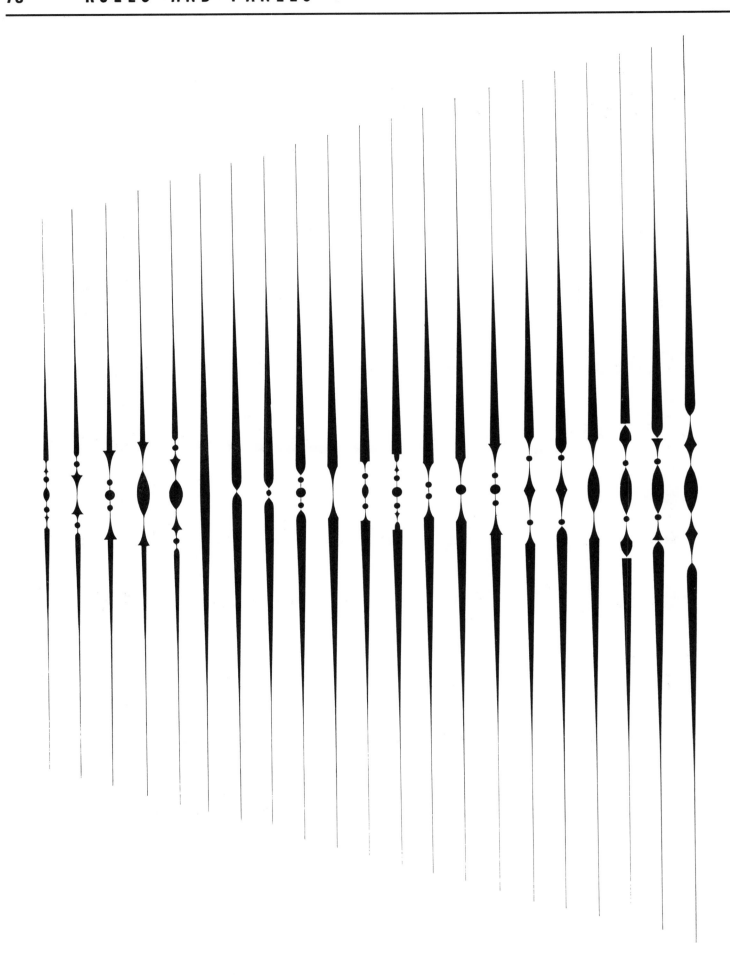

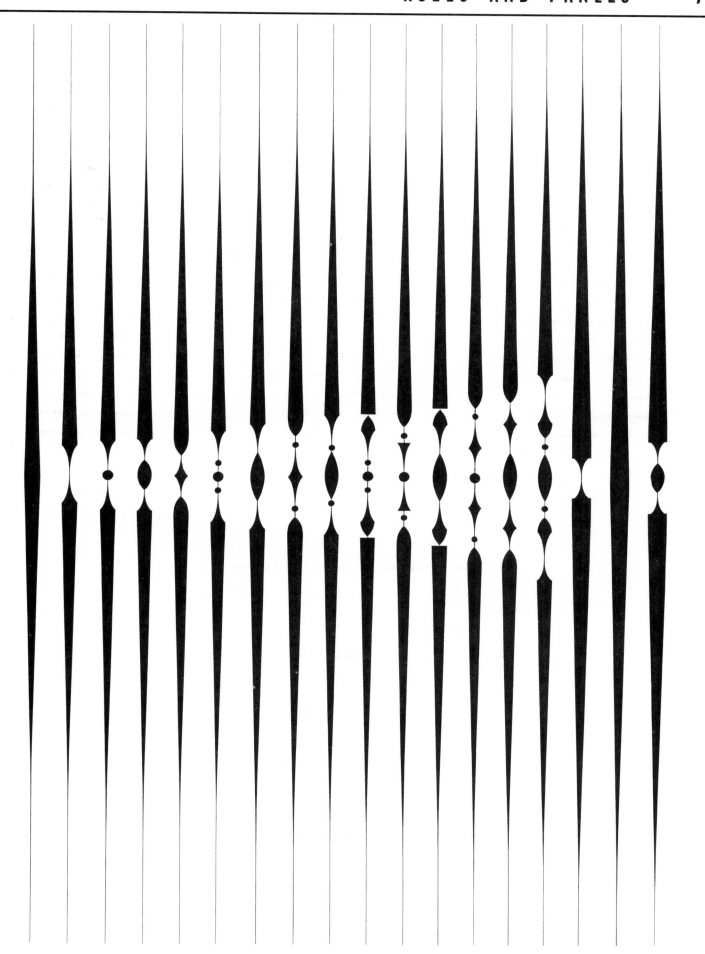

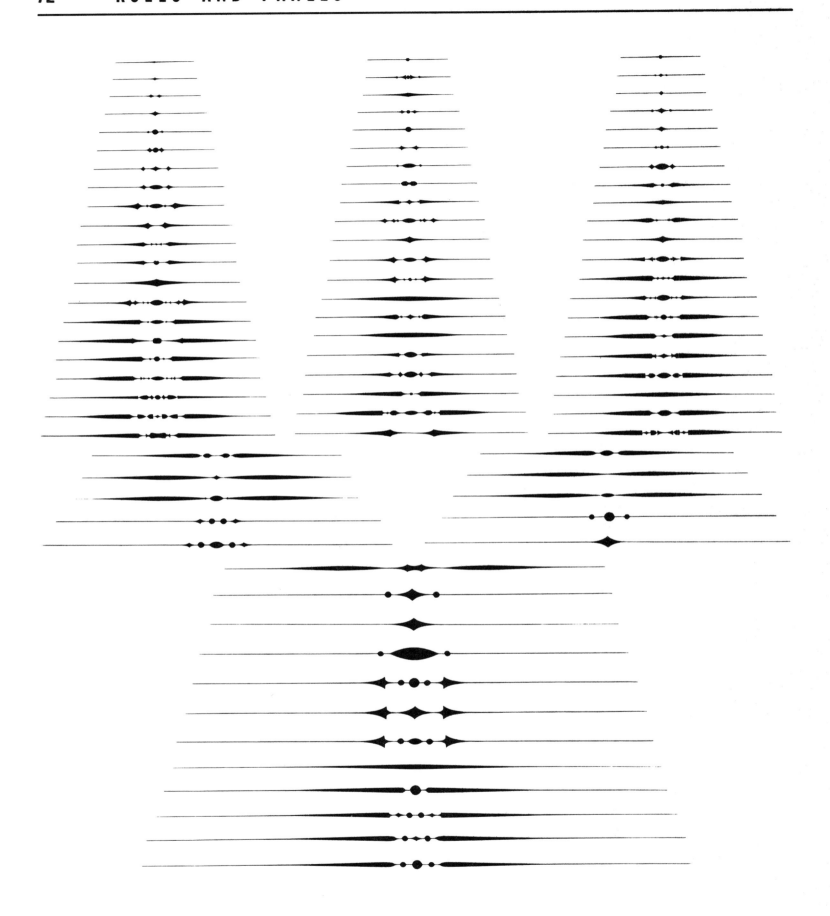

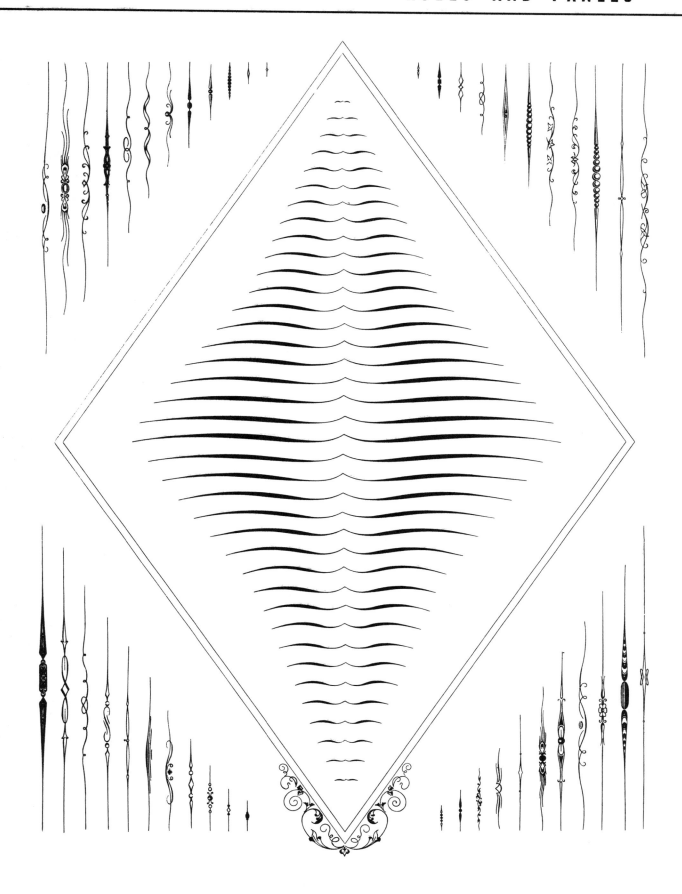

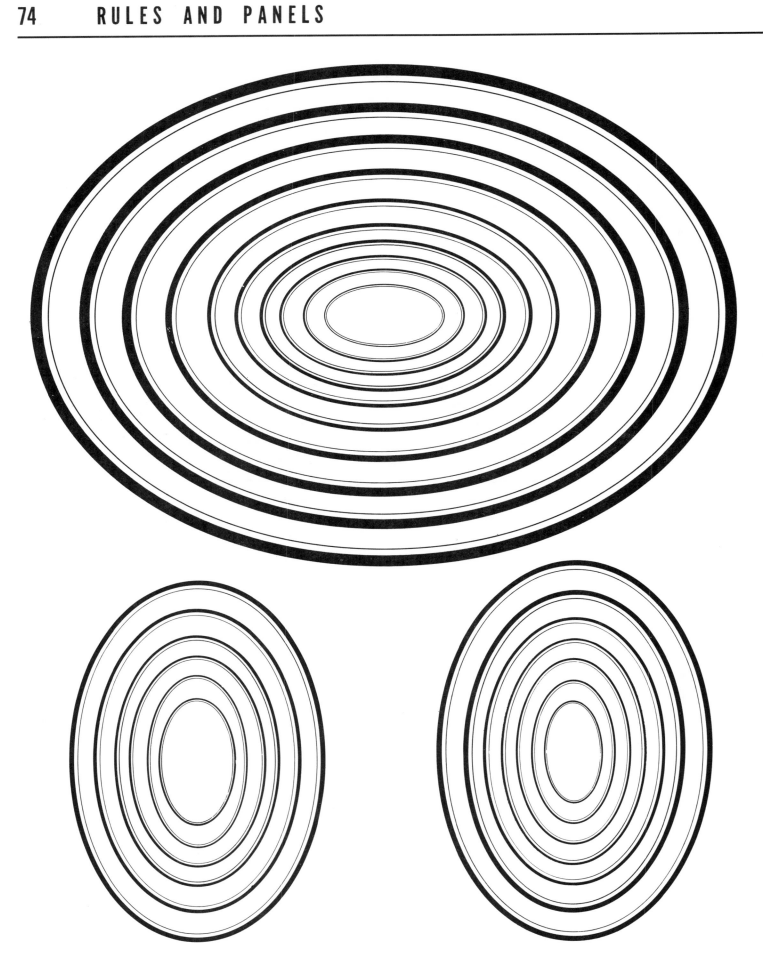

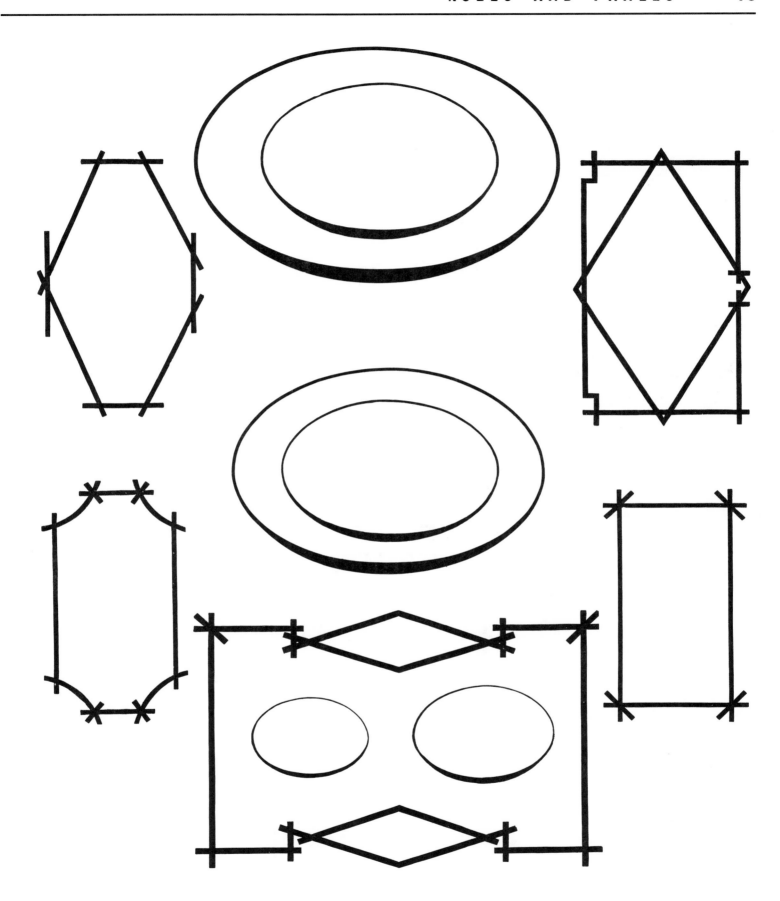

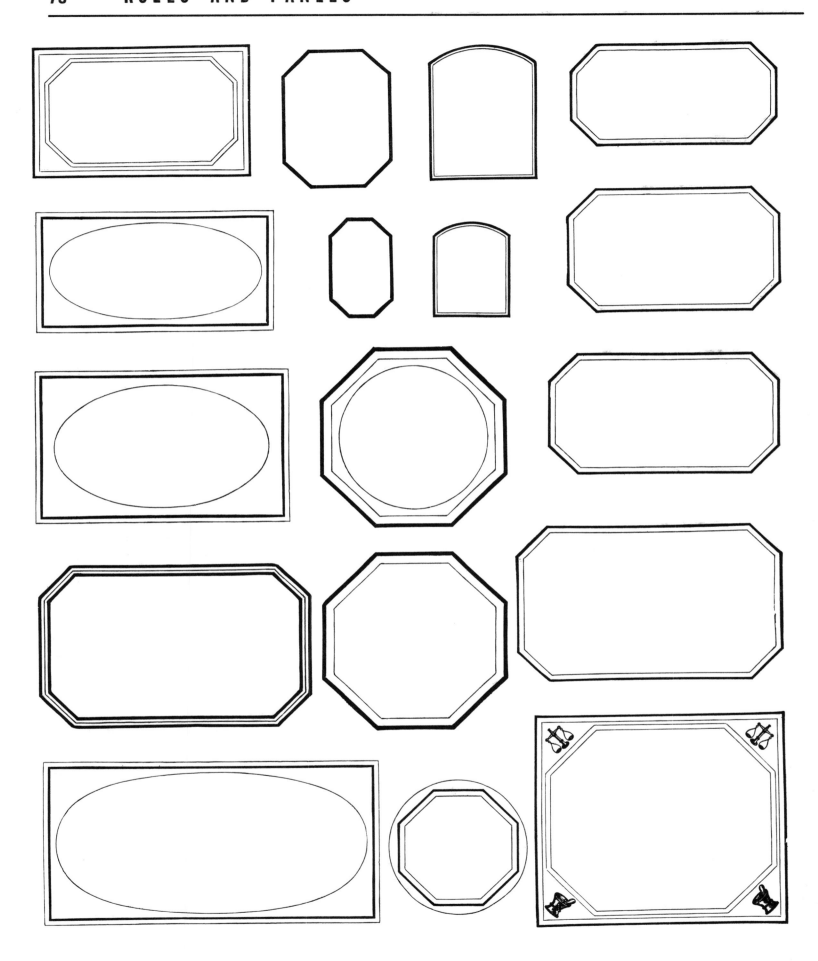

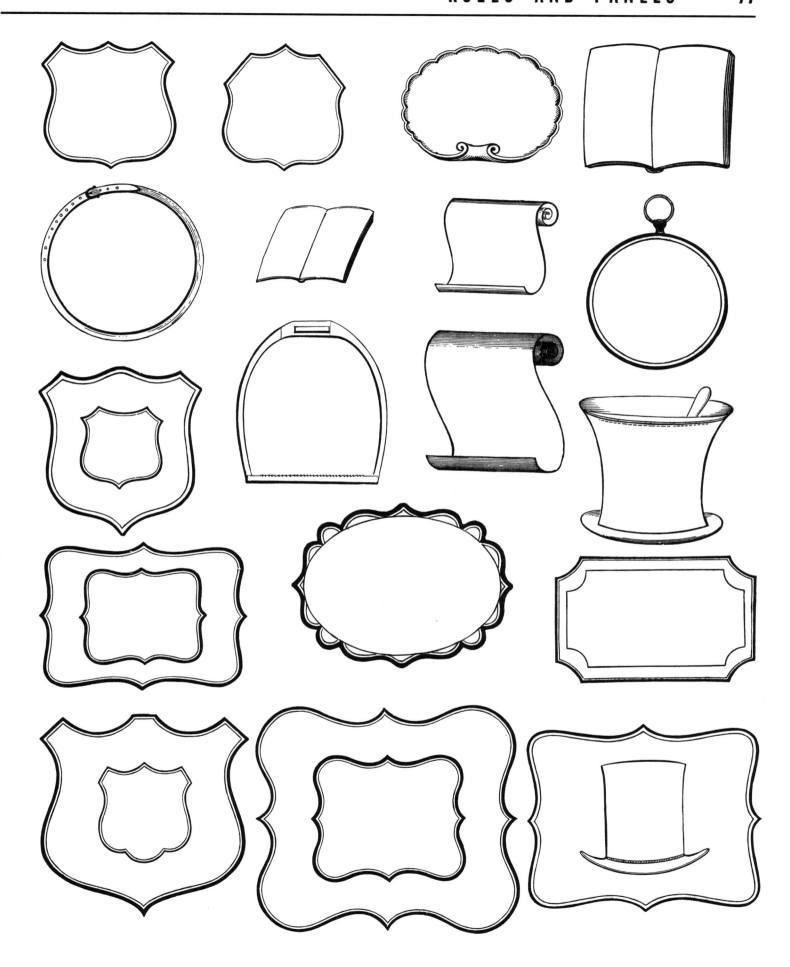

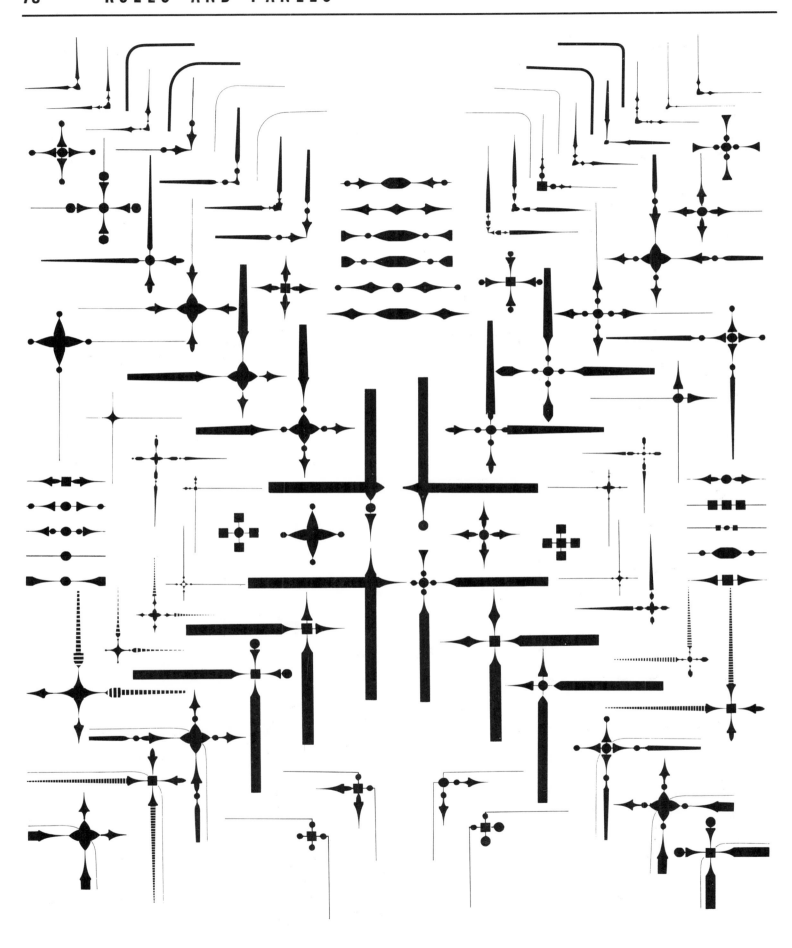

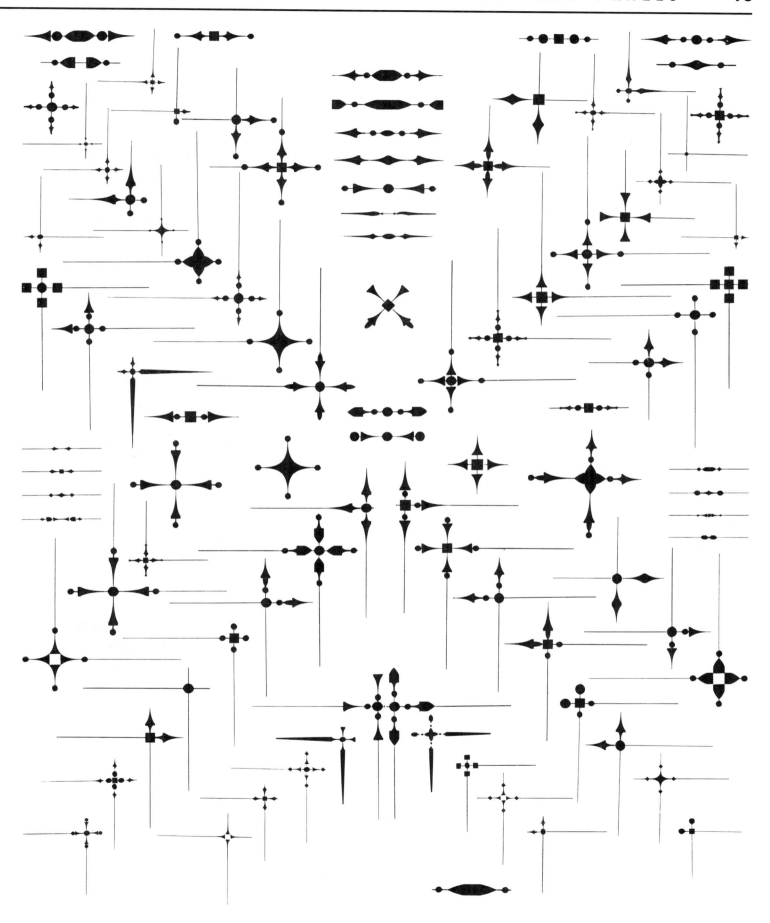

EGYPTIAN✦BORDER

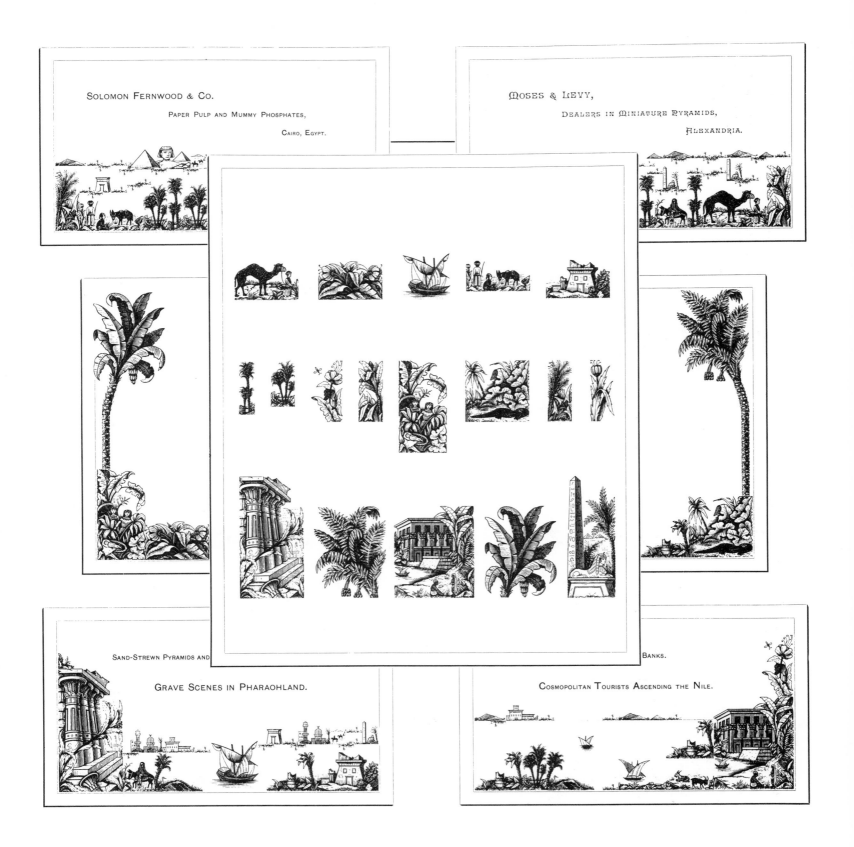

SOLOMON FERNWOOD & CO.

PAPER PULP AND MUMMY PHOSPHATES,

CAIRO, EGYPT.

MOSES & LEVY,

DEALERS IN MINIATURE PYRAMIDS,

ALEXANDRIA.

SAND-STREWN PYRAMIDS AND ... BANKS.

GRAVE SCENES IN PHARAOHLAND.

COSMOPOLITAN TOURISTS ASCENDING THE NILE.

Vintage of the Year 1796

National Holiday

Mortised Ornaments

Betrothal
SAINT VALENTINE'S FESTIVAL

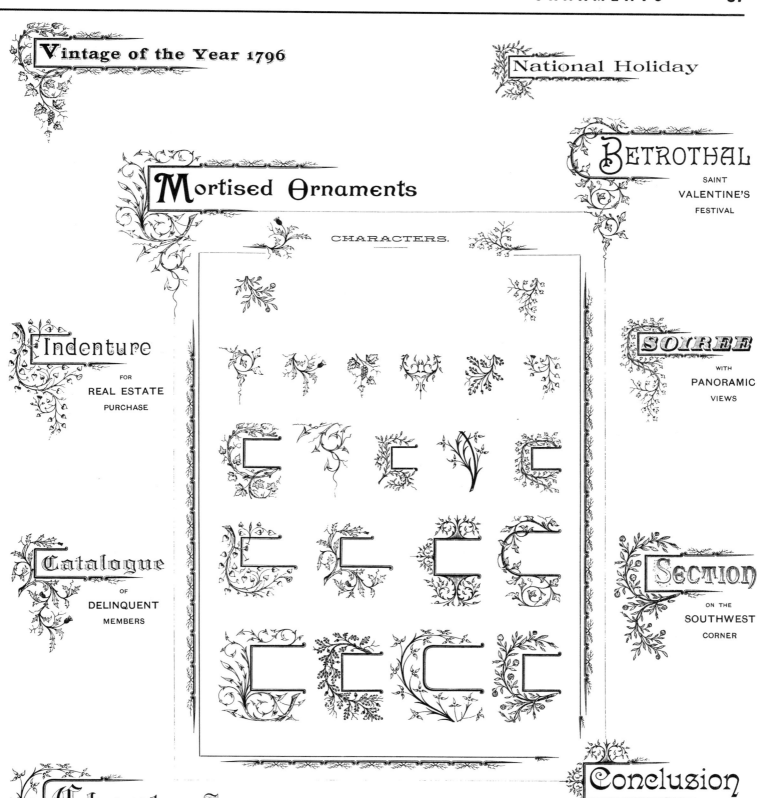

CHARACTERS.

Indenture
FOR REAL ESTATE PURCHASE

Soiree
WITH PANORAMIC VIEWS

Catalogue
OF DELINQUENT MEMBERS

Section
ON THE SOUTHWEST CORNER

Chapter I.

Conclusion

Iron-Bound Buckets
FOR LAWN DECORATIONS

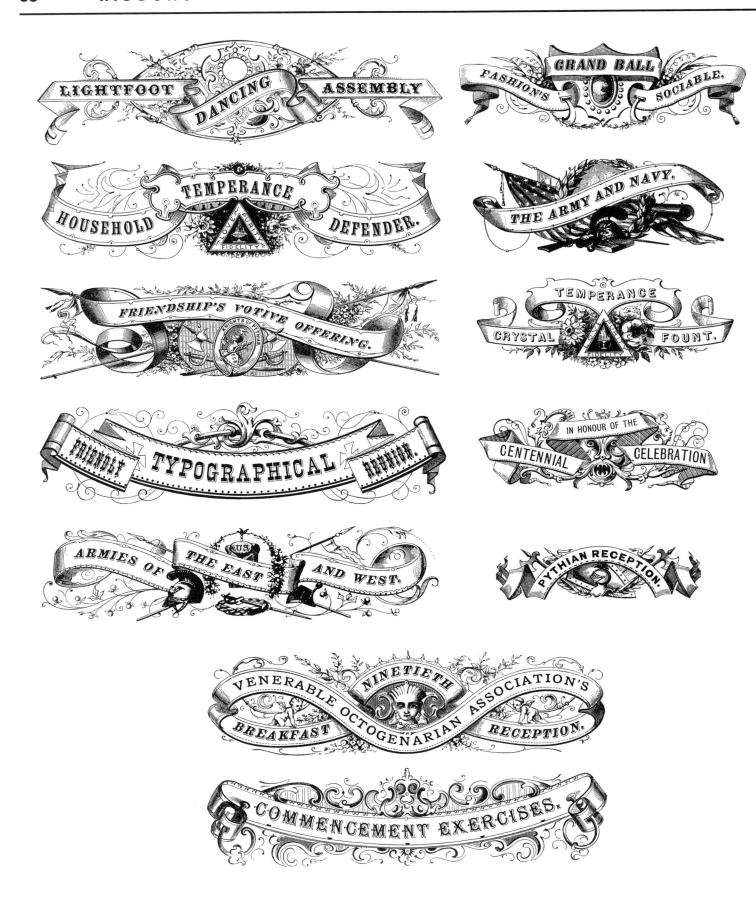

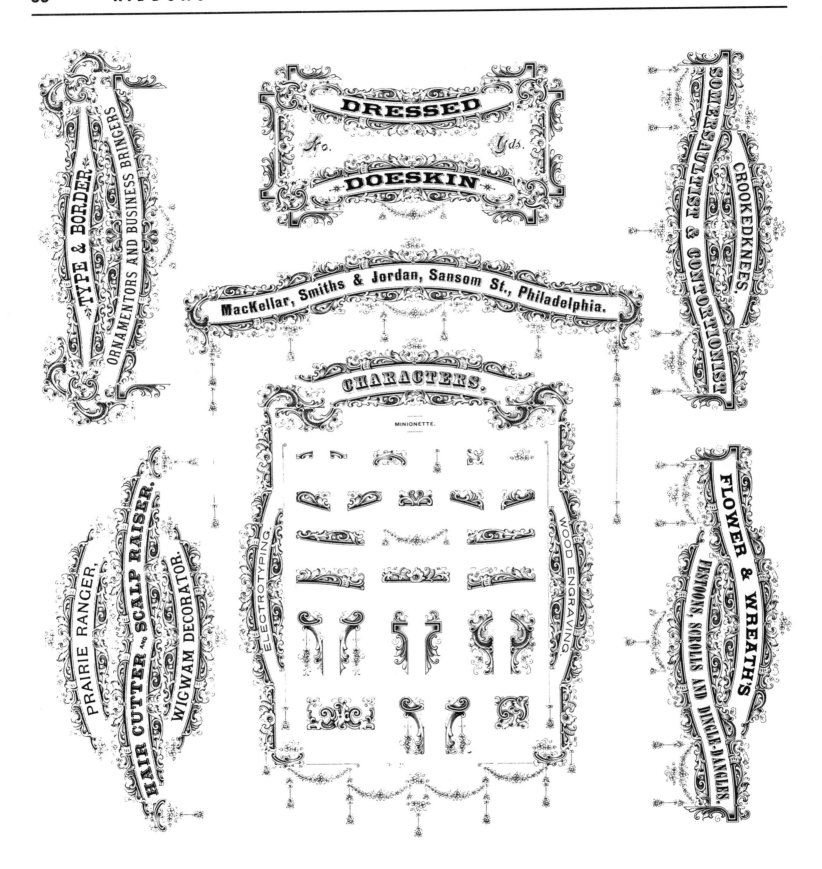

TYPE & BORDER.
ORNAMENTORS AND BUSINESS BRINGERS.

DRESSED
DOESKIN

SOMERSAULTIST & CONTORTIONIST
CROOKEDKNEES.

MacKellar, Smiths & Jordan, Sansom St., Philadelphia.

CHARACTERS.

MINIONETTE.

ELECTROTYPING.

WOOD ENGRAVING.

HAIR CUTTER and SCALP RAISER.
PRAIRIE RANGER,
WIGWAM DECORATOR.

FLOWER & WREATH'S
FESTOONS, SCROLLS AND DINGLE-DANGLES.

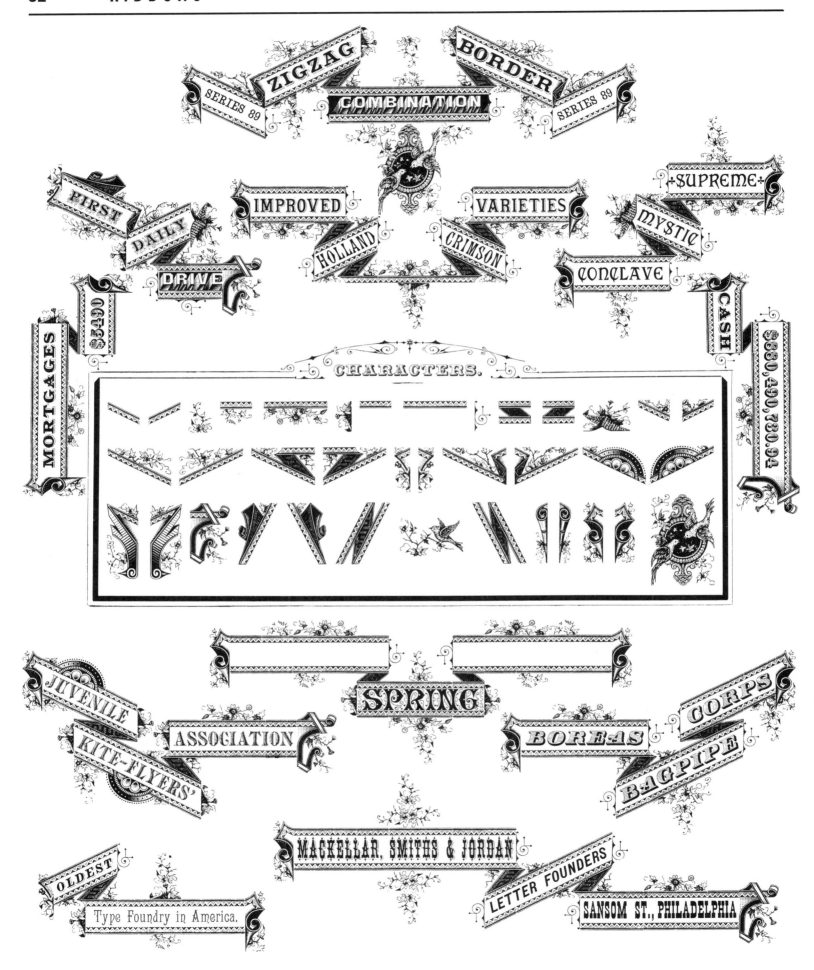

ZIGZAG BORDER
SERIES 89   COMBINATION   SERIES 89

FIRST IMPROVED VARIETIES SUPREME
DAILY HOLLAND CRIMSON MYSTIC
DRIVE CONCLAVE

MORTGAGES $5400   CHARACTERS.   CASH $680,490,730.94

SPRING
JUVENILE ASSOCIATION BOREAS CORPS
KITE-FLYERS' BAGPIPE

OLDEST   MACKELLAR, SMITHS & JORDAN
Type Foundry in America.   LETTER FOUNDERS   SANSOM ST., PHILADELPHIA

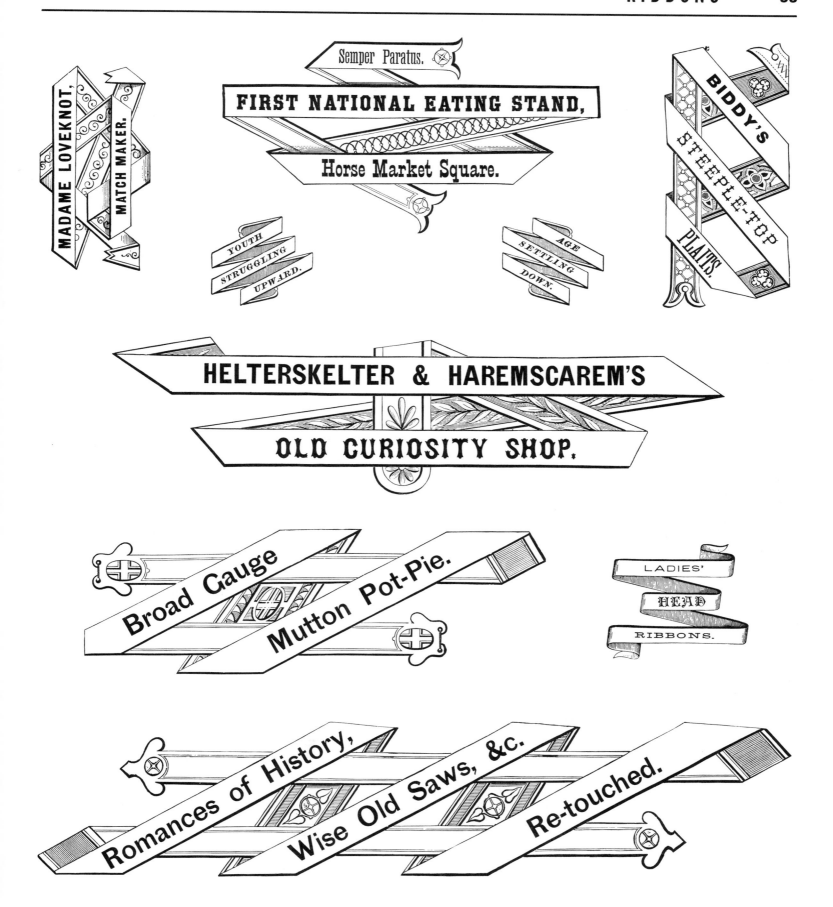

Semper Paratus.

FIRST NATIONAL EATING STAND,

Horse Market Square.

MADAME LOVEKNOT, MATCH MAKER.

YOUTH STRUGGLING UPWARD.

AGE SETTLING DOWN.

BIDDY'S STEEPLE-TOP PLAITS.

HELTERSKELTER & HAREMSCAREM'S

OLD CURIOSITY SHOP.

Broad Gauge Mutton Pot-Pie.

LADIES' HEAD RIBBONS.

Romances of History, Wise Old Saws, &c. Re-touched.

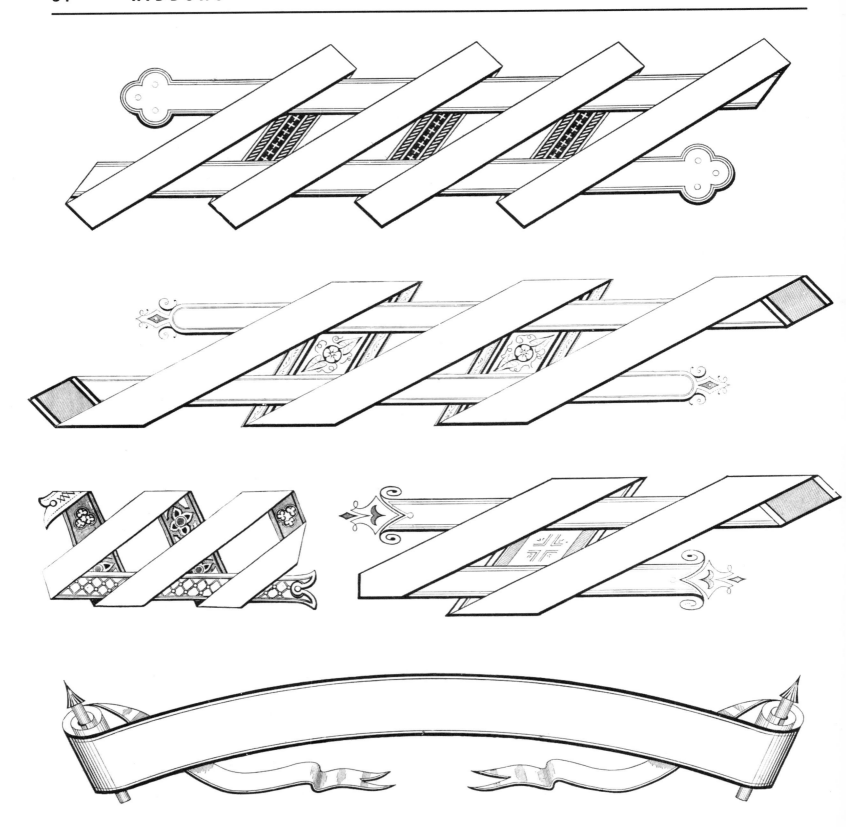

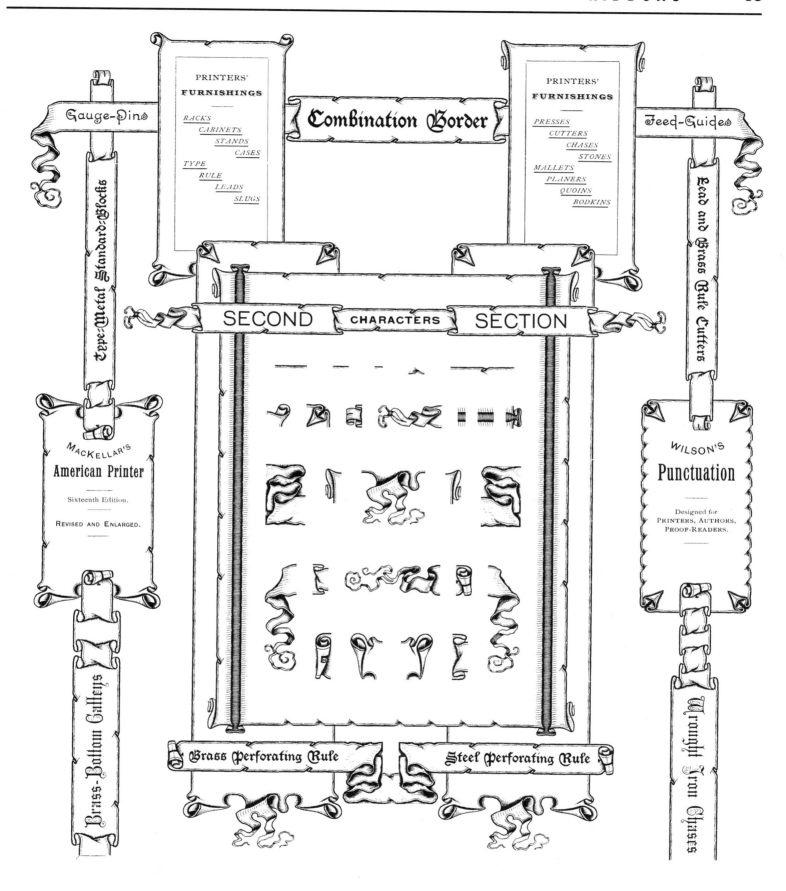

Gauge-Pins

Feed-Guides

PRINTERS'
FURNISHINGS

RACKS
CABINETS
STANDS
CASES

TYPE
RULE
LEADS
SLUGS

PRINTERS'
FURNISHINGS

PRESSES
CUTTERS
CHASES
STONES

MALLETS
PLANERS
QUOINS
BODKINS

Combination Border

Type-Metal Standard-Blocks

Lead and Brass Rule Cutters

SECOND CHARACTERS SECTION

MacKellar's
American Printer

Sixteenth Edition.

REVISED AND ENLARGED.

WILSON'S
Punctuation

Designed for
PRINTERS, AUTHORS,
PROOF-READERS.

Brass-Bottom Galleys

Wrought Iron Chases

Brass Perforating Rule

Steel Perforating Rule

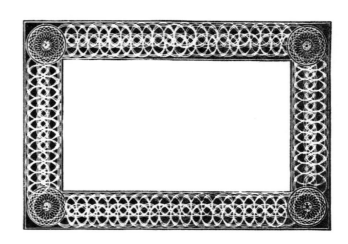

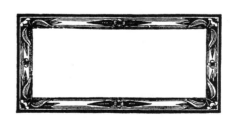

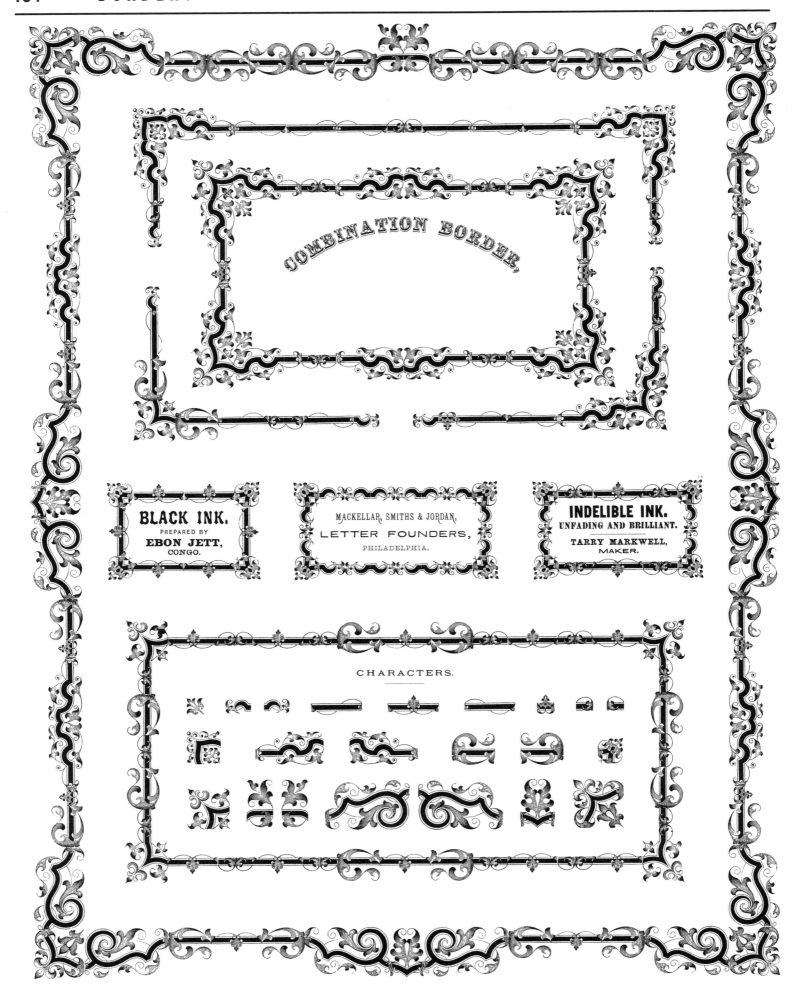

COMBINATION BORDER.

BLACK INK.
PREPARED BY
EBON JETT,
CONGO.

MACKELLAR, SMITHS & JORDAN,
LETTER FOUNDERS,
PHILADELPHIA.

INDELIBLE INK.
UNFADING AND BRILLIANT.
TARRY MARKWELL,
MAKER.

CHARACTERS.

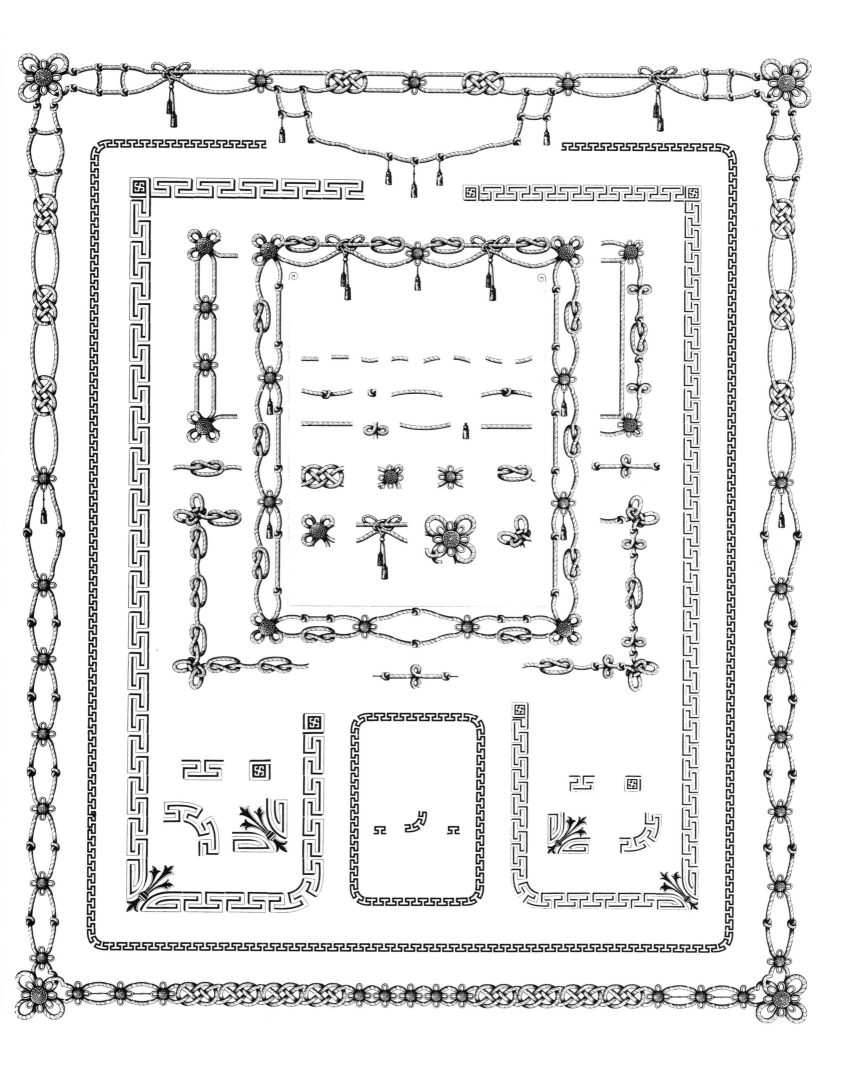

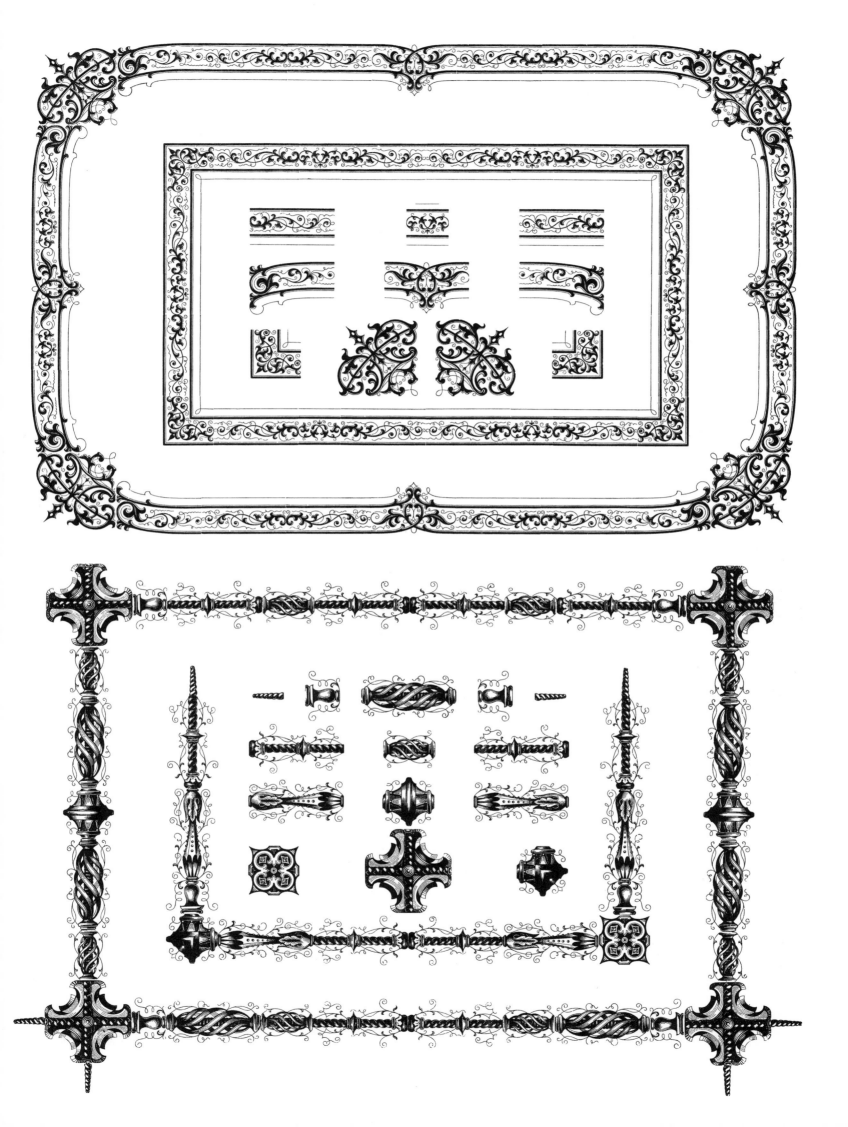

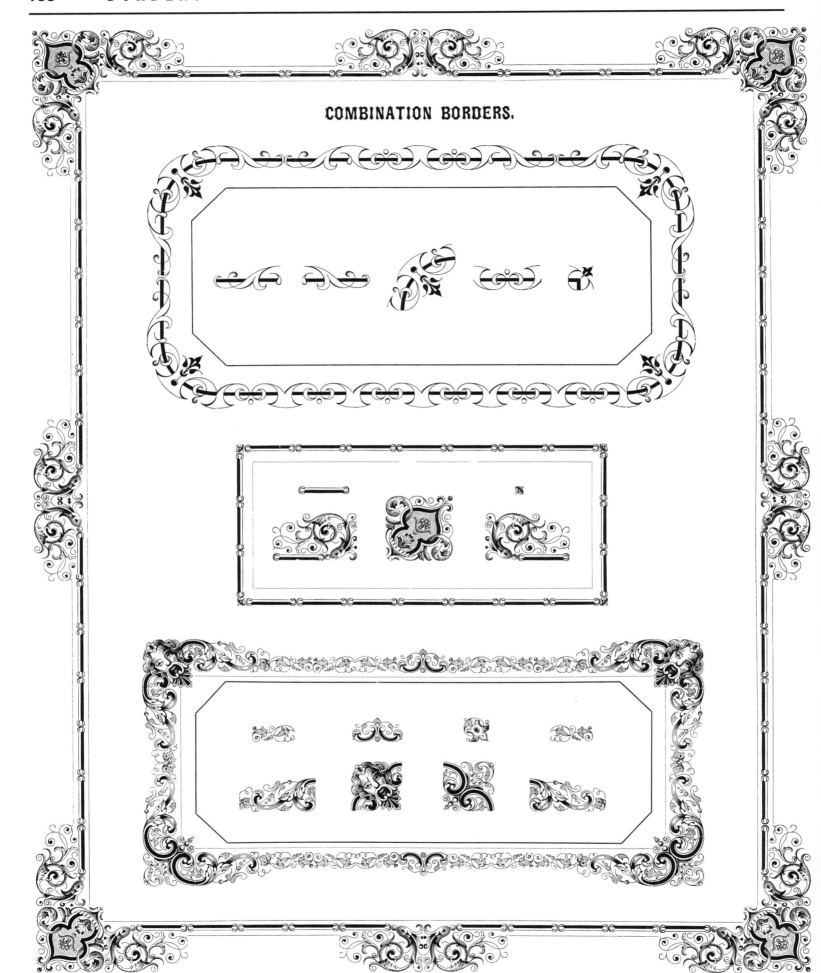

COMBINATION BORDERS.

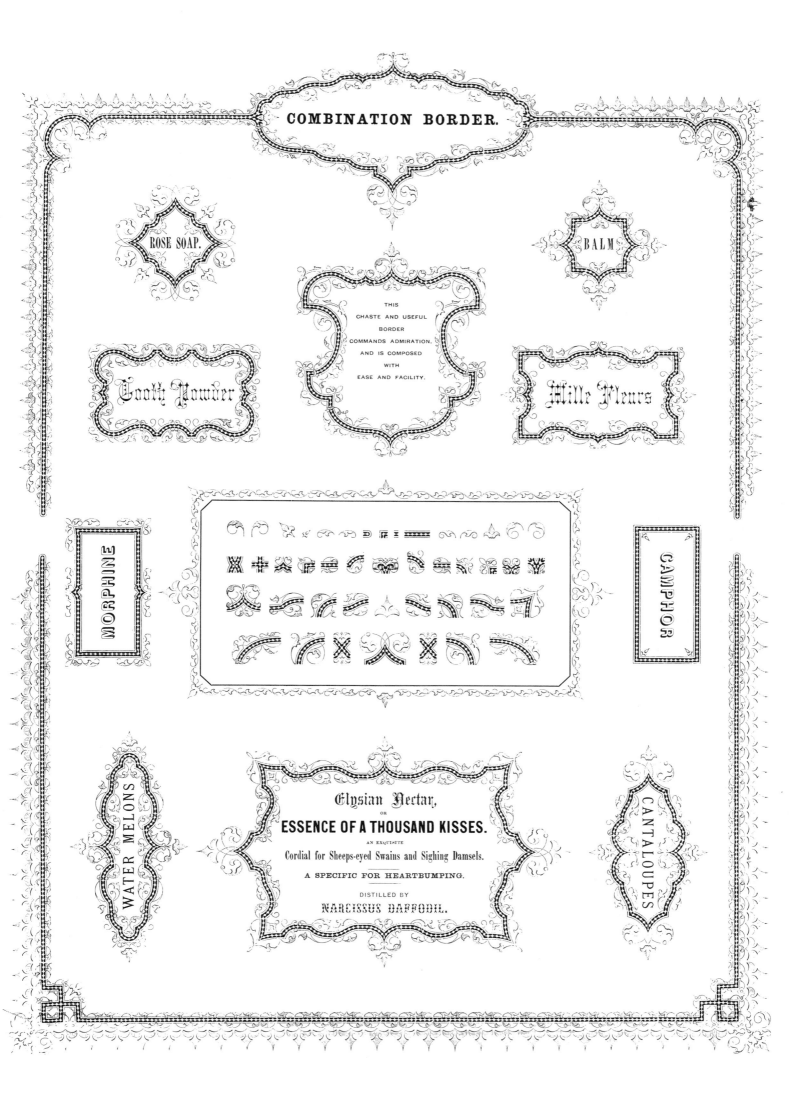

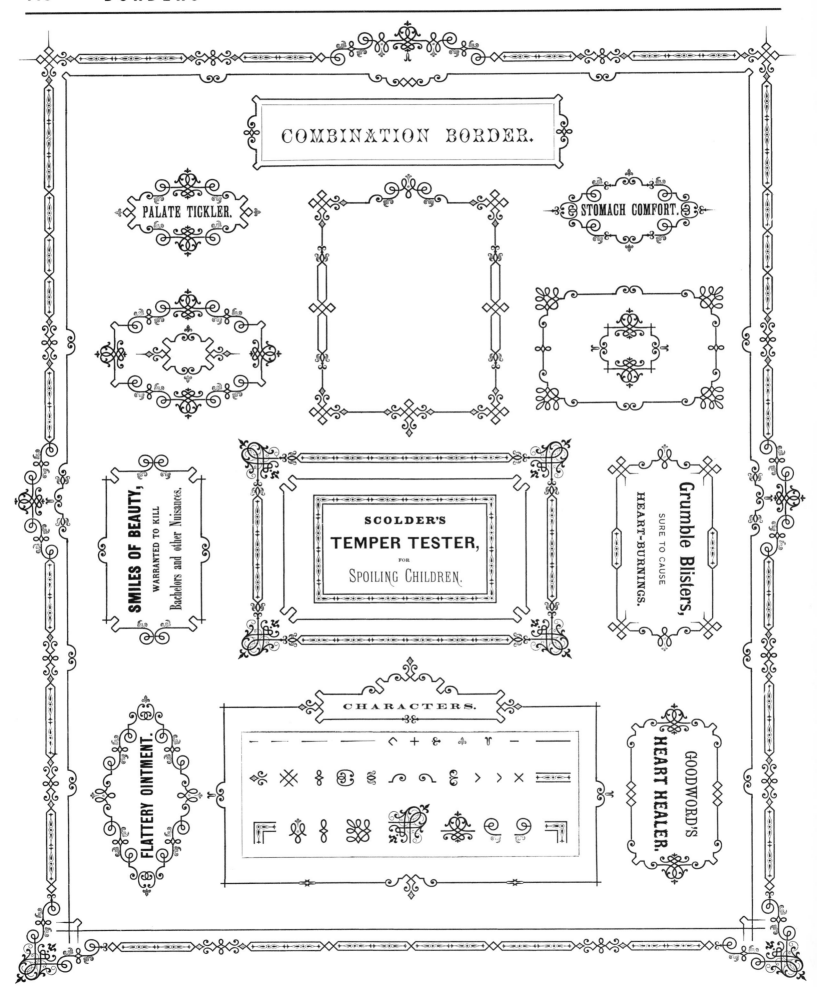

COMBINATION BORDER.

PALATE TICKLER.

STOMACH COMFORT.

SMILES OF BEAUTY,
WARRANTED TO KILL
Bachelors and other Nuisances.

SCOLDER'S
TEMPER TESTER,
FOR
Spoiling Children.

Grumble Blisters,
SURE TO CAUSE
HEART-BURNINGS.

FLATTERY OINTMENT.

CHARACTERS.

GOODWORD'S
HEART HEALER.

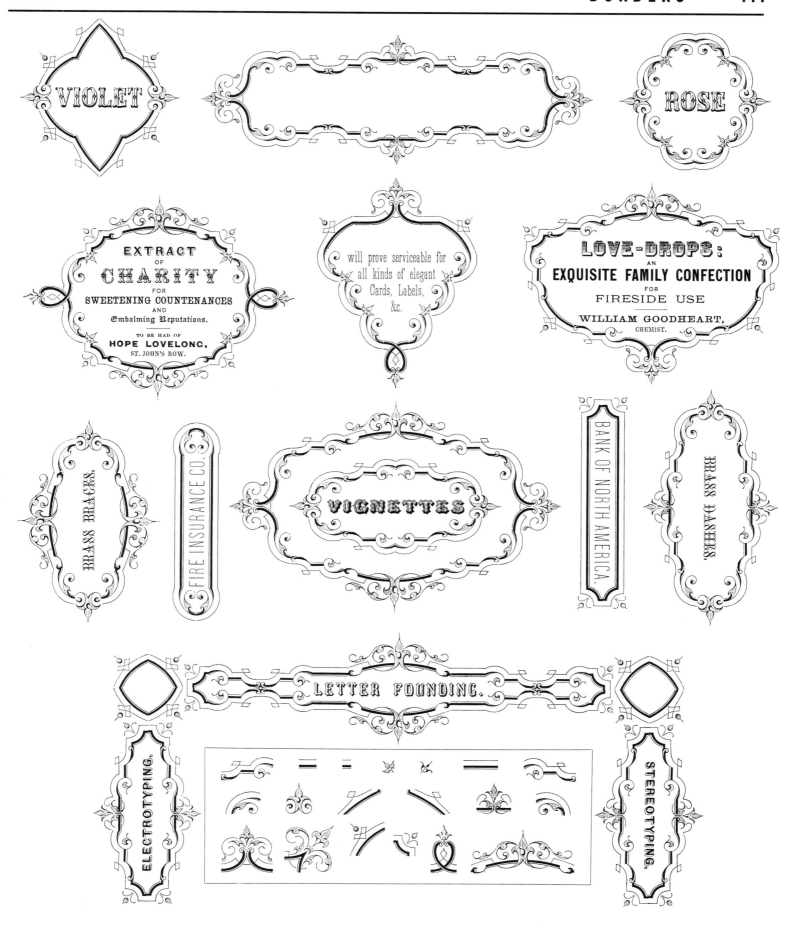

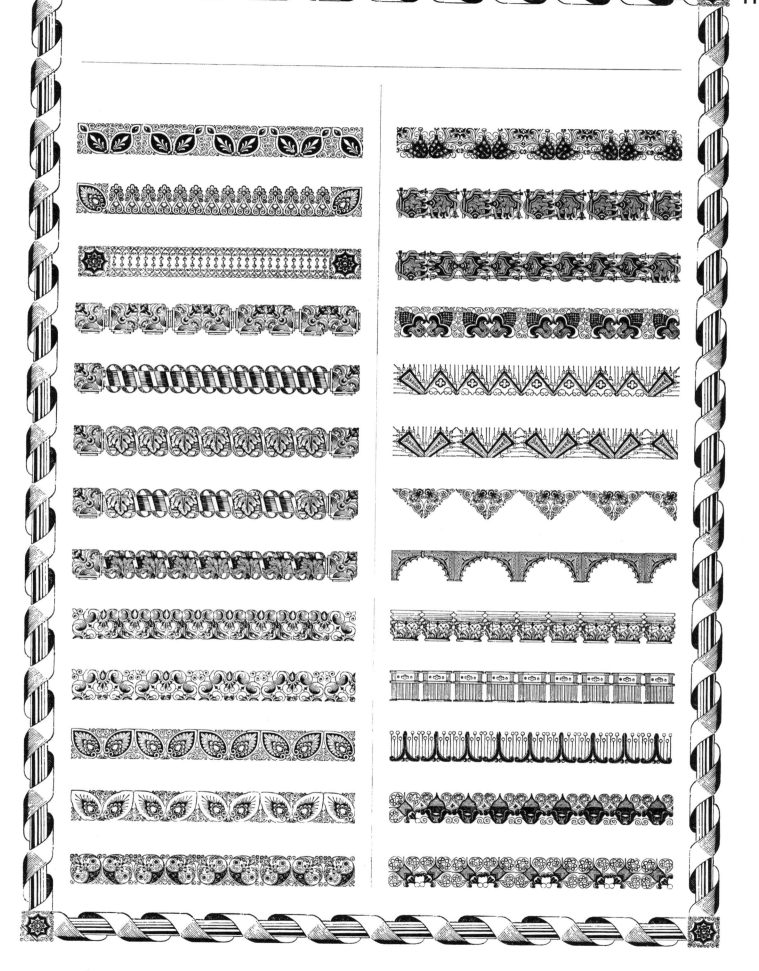

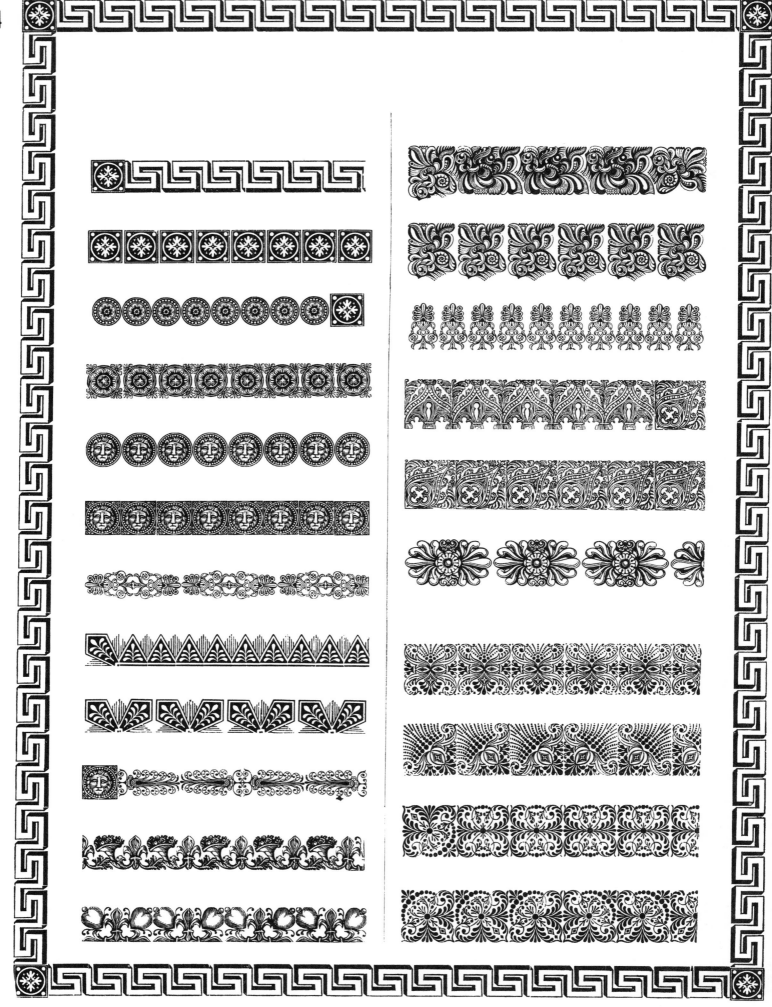

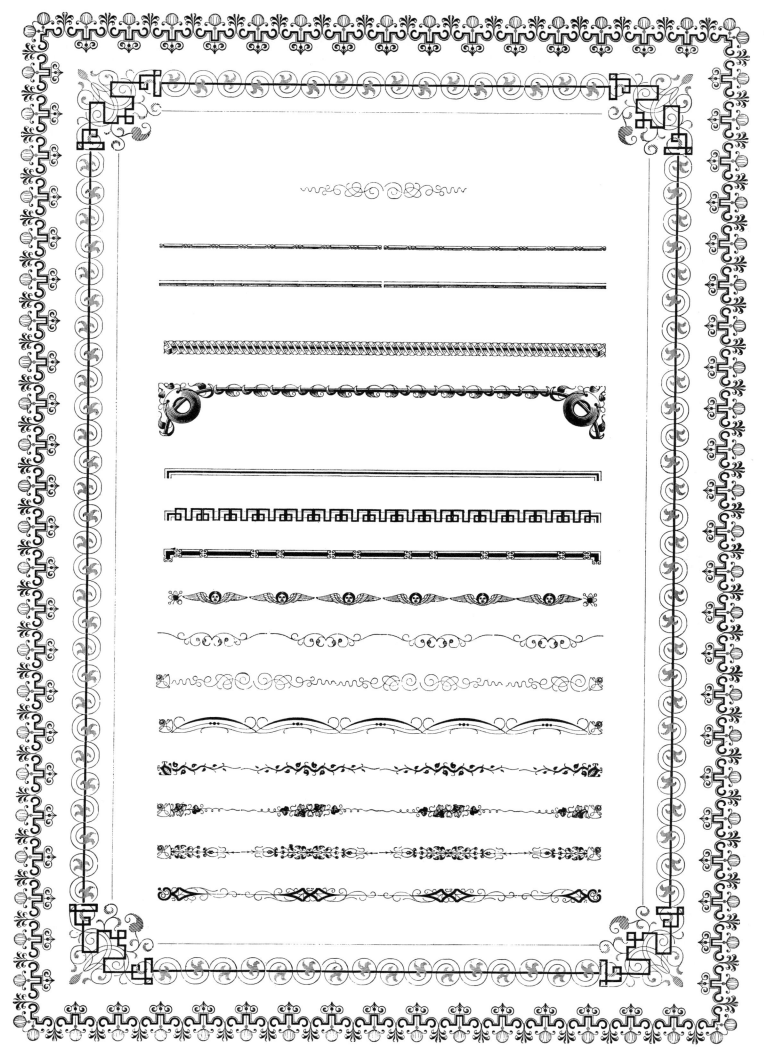

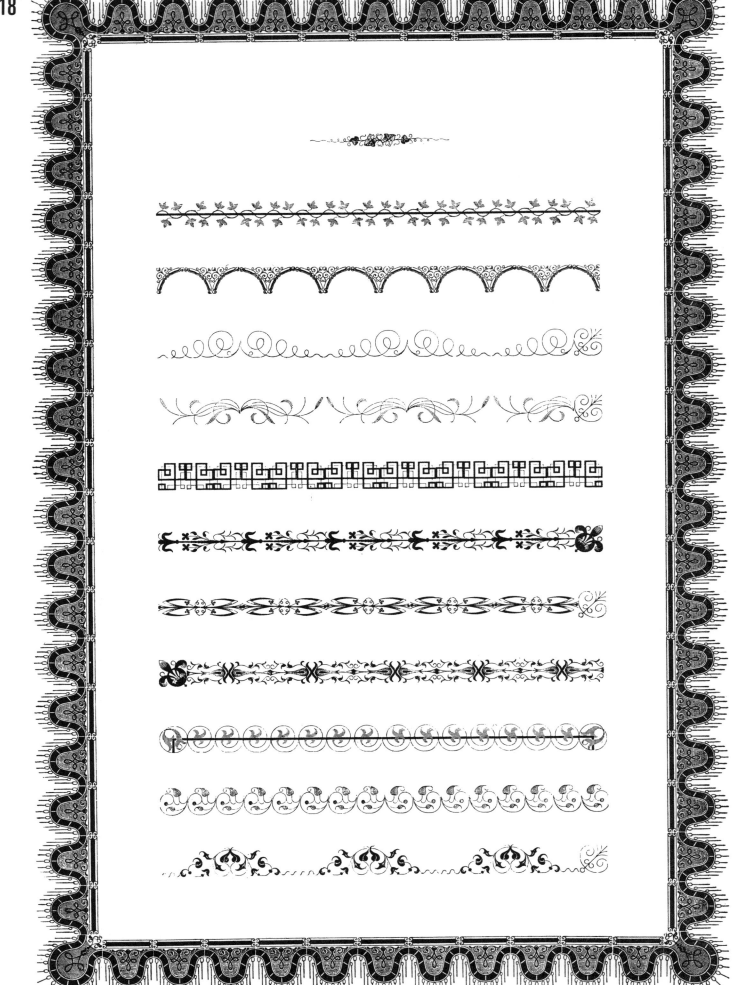

118

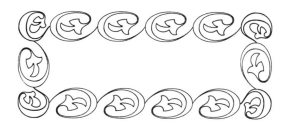

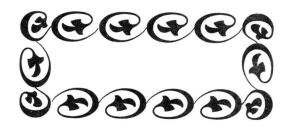

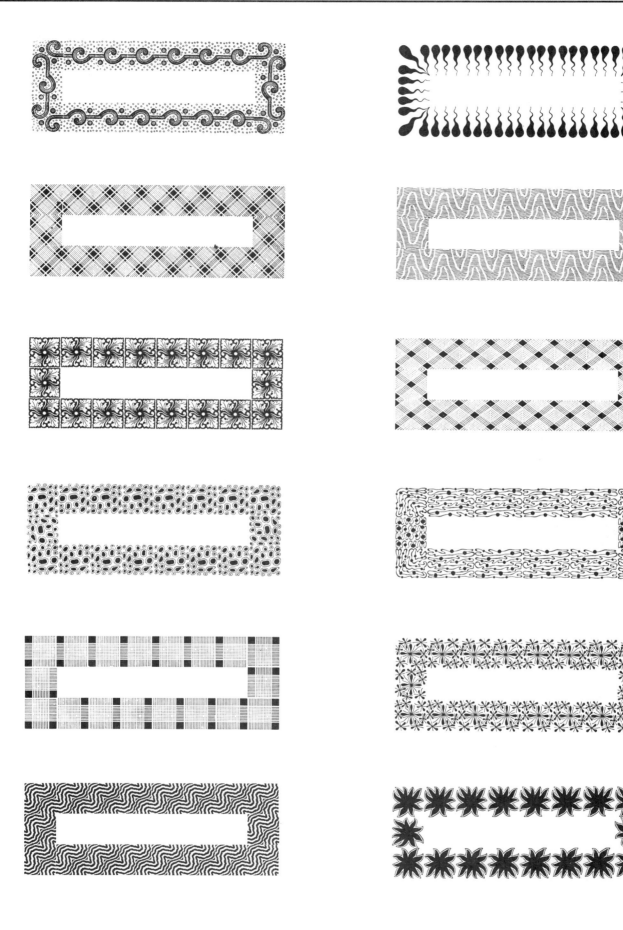

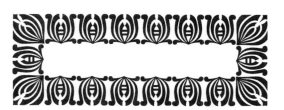

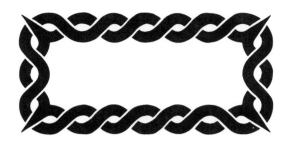

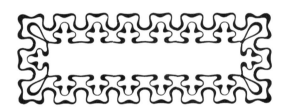
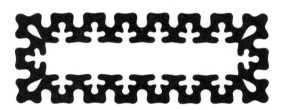

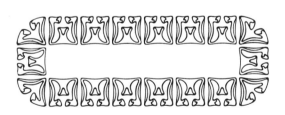

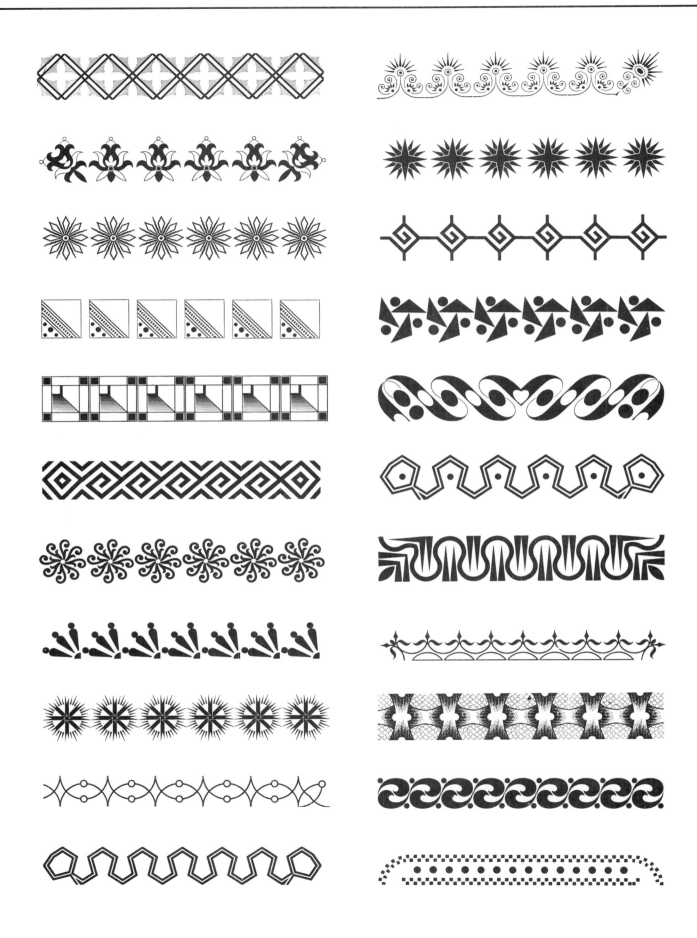

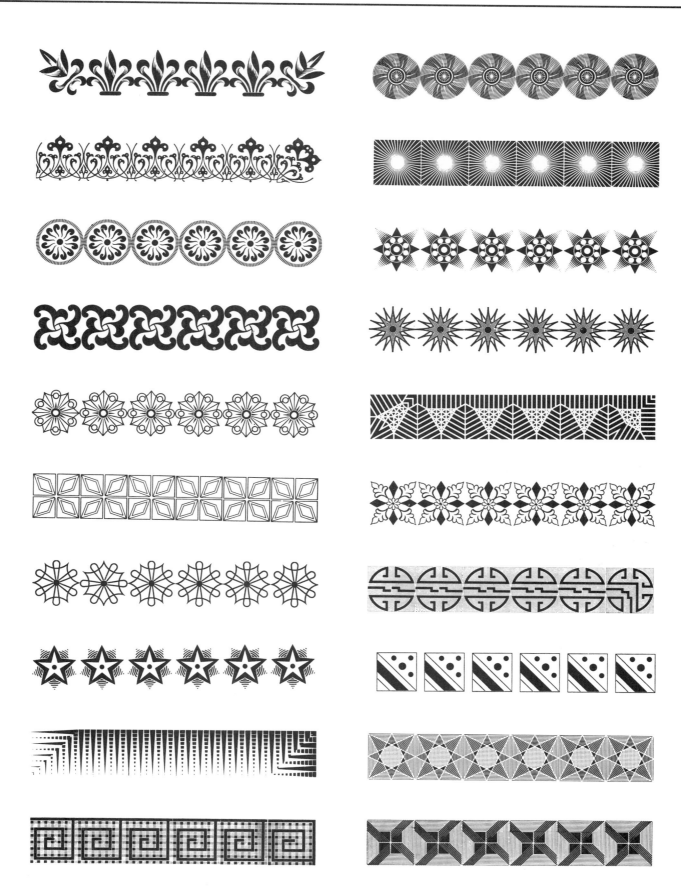

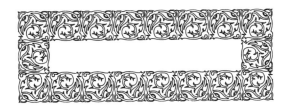

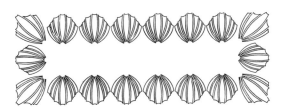

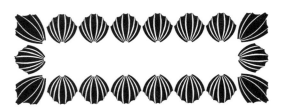

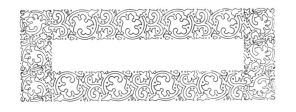

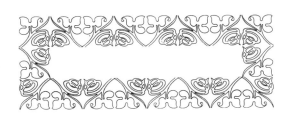

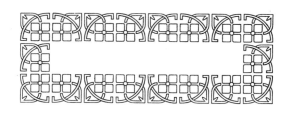

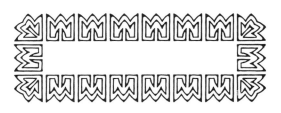

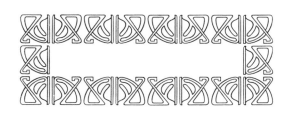

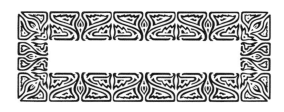

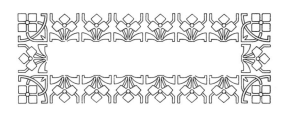

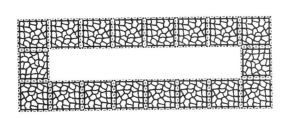

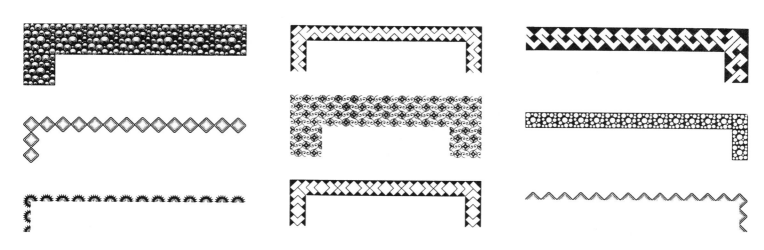

BORDER GEMS.

CHARACTERS.

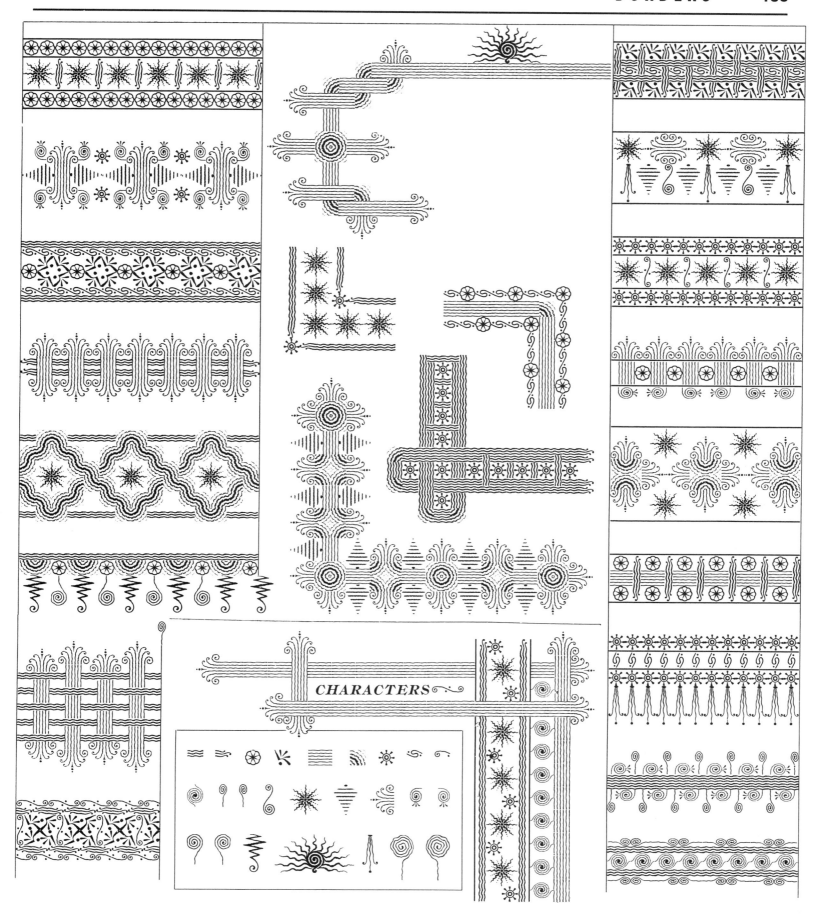

CHARACTERS

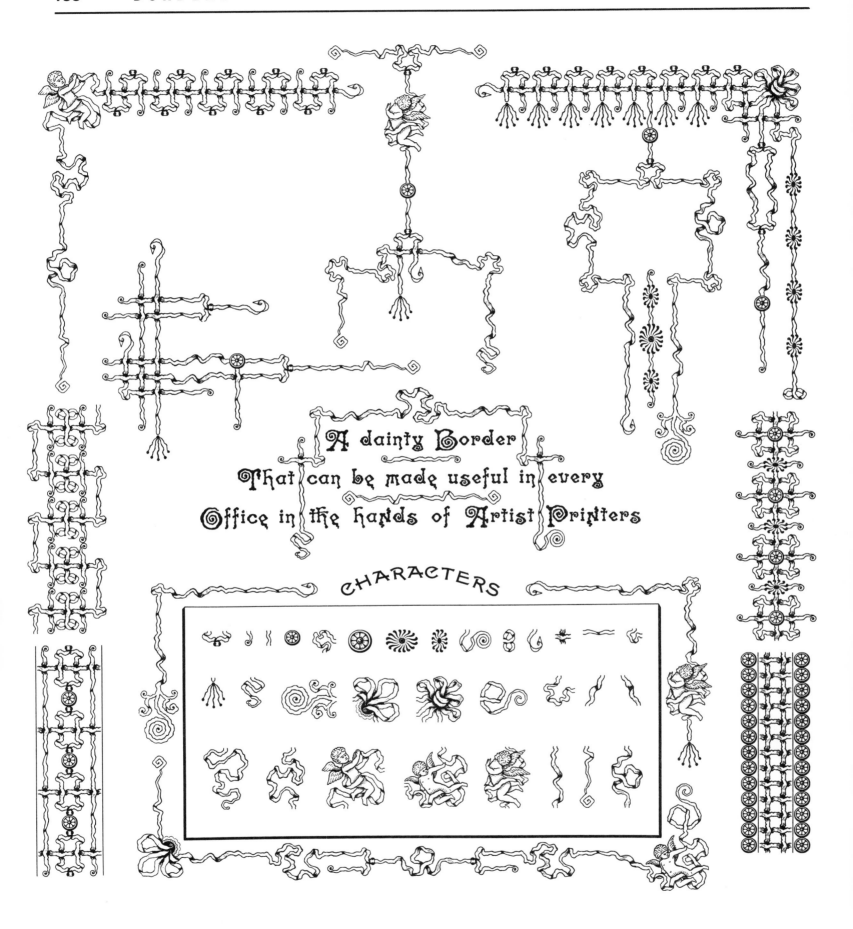

A dainty Border
That can be made useful in every
Office in the hands of Artist Printers

CHARACTERS

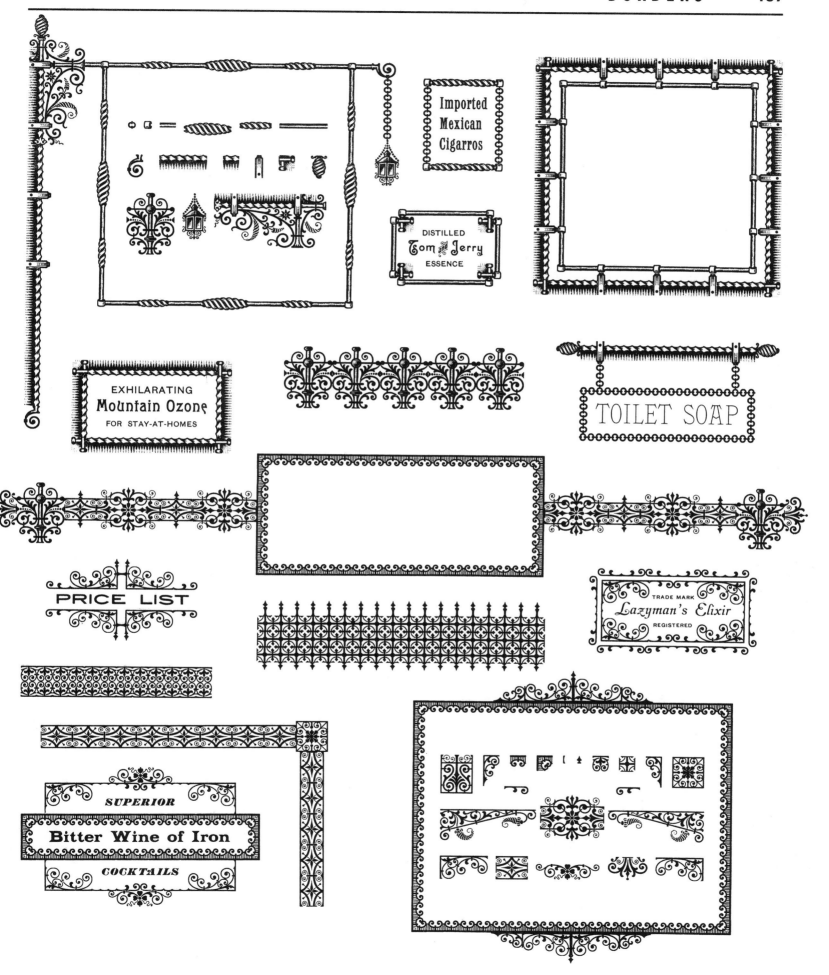

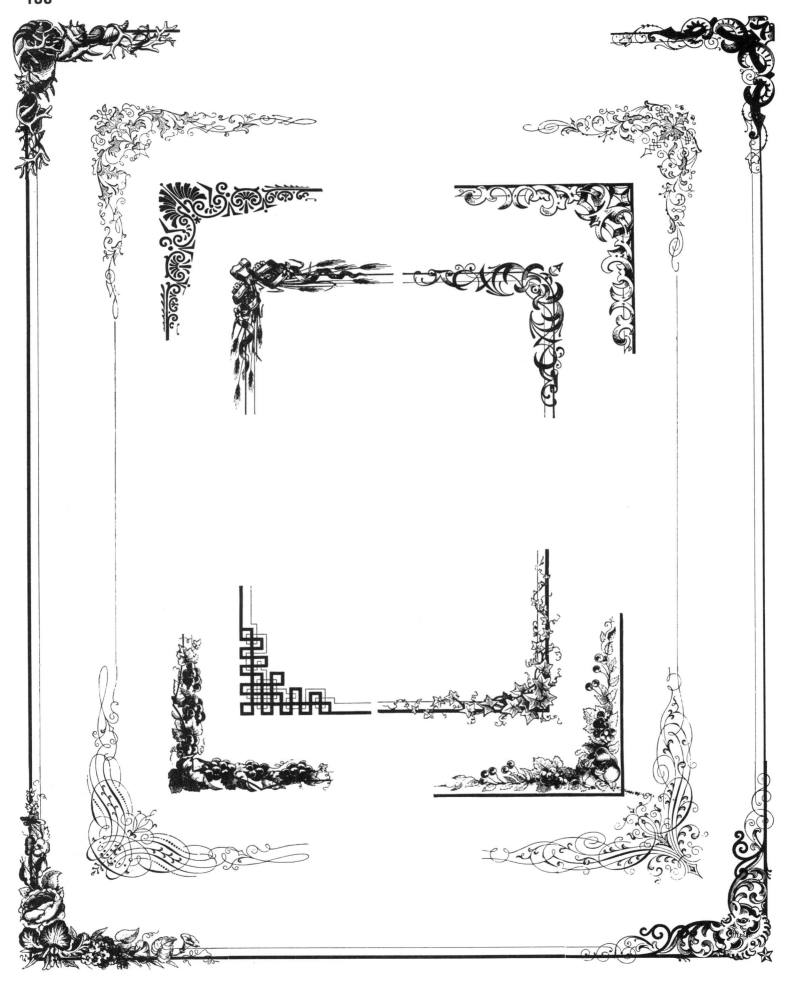

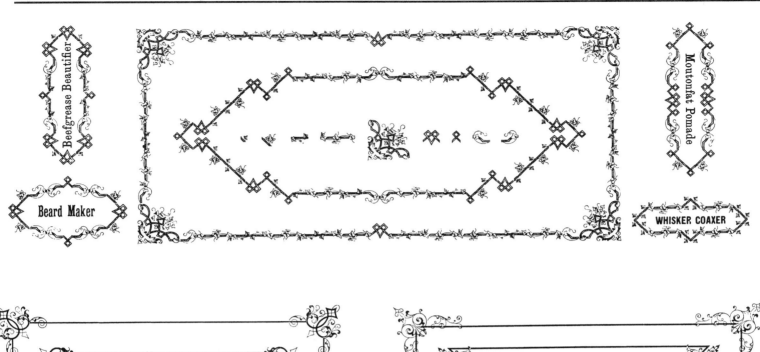

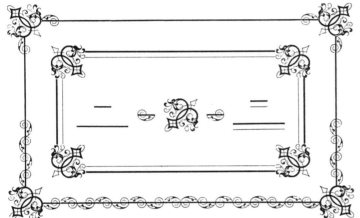

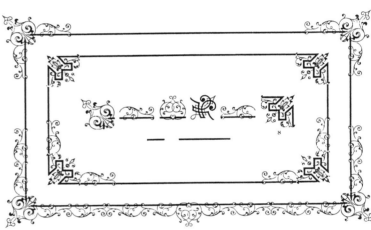

SNAPPER SAUCE.

CONCENTRATED
Essence of Sirloin.
AN ADMIRABLE
STOMACH STRENGTHENER.

COURTESY LOZENGES.

CONDENSED
PLUM PUDDING.
Good for Young Bulls.

MAGIC
TRUTH DROPS,
A Prophylactic for
CONSCIENCE STINGS
WARRANTED.

Temper Sauce.

COMBINATION BORDER.

Slander Spice.

ESSENCE
OF
CIVILITY
GOOD AT ALL TIMES
FOR
PERT MISSES
AND
Airish Youngsters.

CHARACTERS.

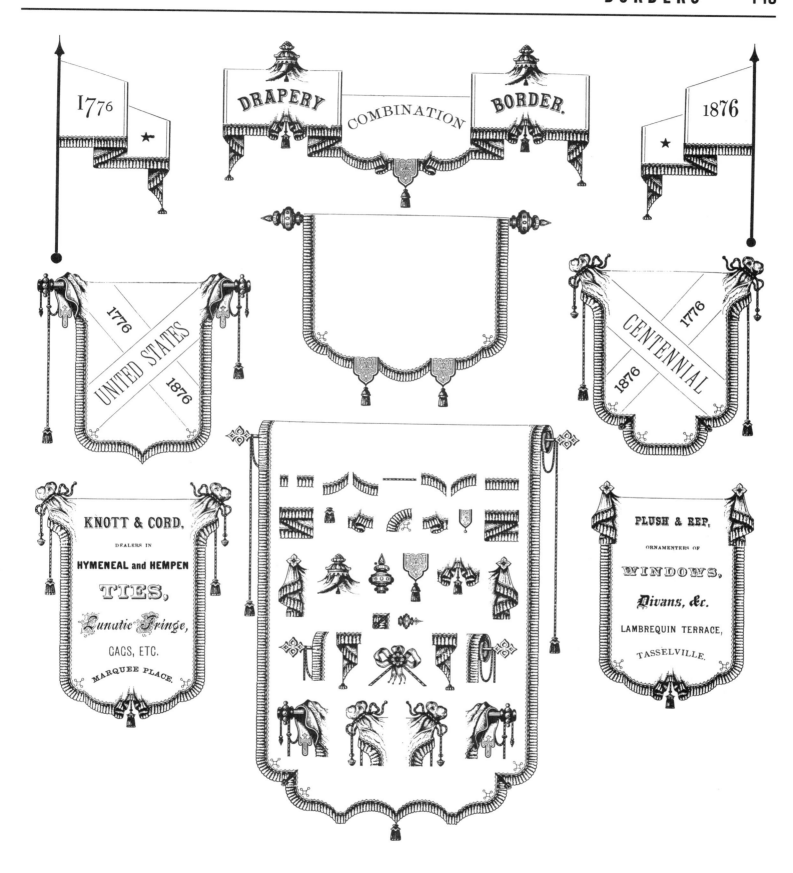

1776

DRAPERY COMBINATION BORDER.

1876

1776 UNITED STATES 1876

CENTENNIAL 1776 1876

KNOTT & CORD,

DEALERS IN

HYMENEAL and HEMPEN

TIES,

Lunatic Fringe,

GAGS, ETC.

MARQUEE PLACE.

PLUSH & REP,

ORNAMENTERS OF

WINDOWS,

Divans, &c.

LAMBREQUIN TERRACE,

TASSELVILLE.

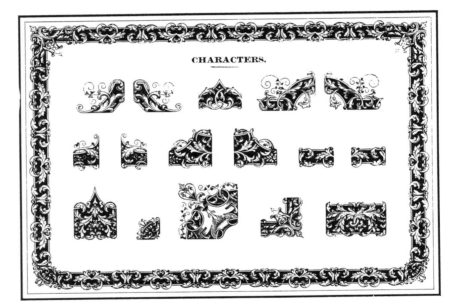

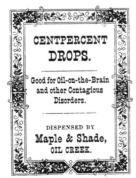

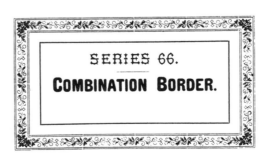

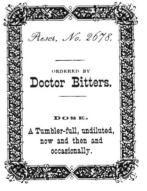

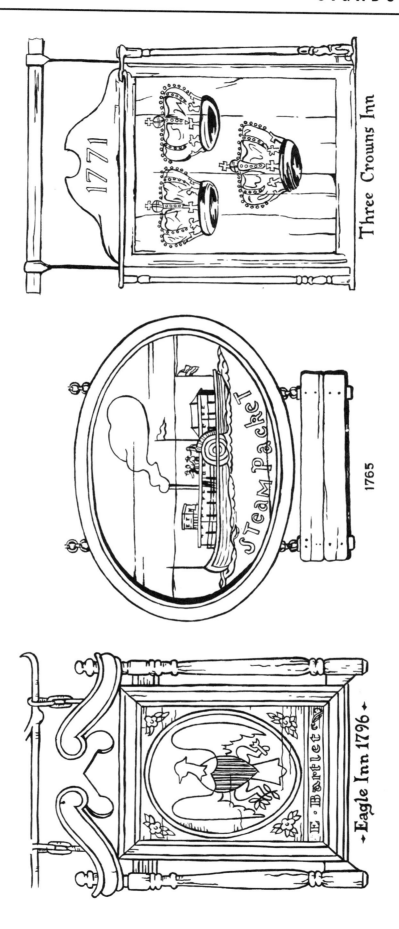

Three Crowns Inn

1765

Eagle Inn 1796

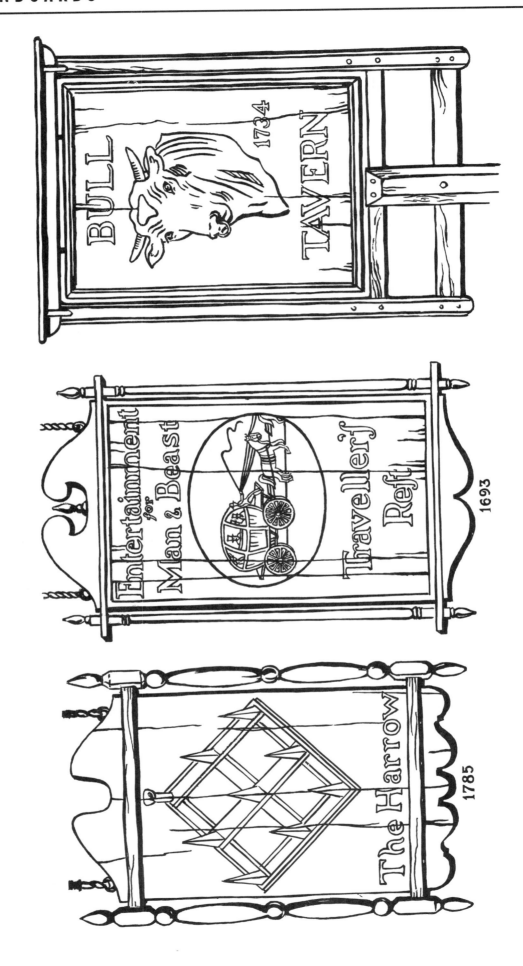

THE RED LION INN
FOUNDED 1730

Cross Keys Hotel
HOTEL
1745

The Beehive
1760
Entertainment By.
A. Walker

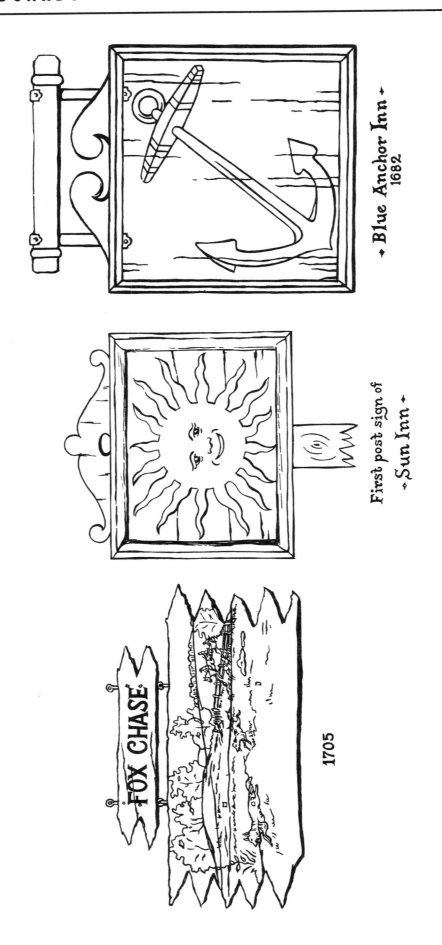

• Blue Anchor Inn •
1682

First post sign of
• Sun Inn •

FOX CHASE

1705

The major sources of illustrations are type specimen books prior to 1890. Because the illustrations appear frequently in different catalogues and different years, the publisher believes that no useful or scholarly purpose is served by giving the exact source since no effort was made to reproduce or investigate their first appearance.

The following specimen catalogues were the main sources for this collection:

MacKellar, Smiths and Jordan.

White, John T. NEW YORK TYPE FOUNDRY SPECIMEN OF PRINTING TYPES CAST.

A. Zeese and Company.

James Conner's Sons.

Blomgren and Co.

Phelps Dalton and Co.

The following sources were also used:

Scrapbooks of the works of Dr. Alexander Anderson in the New York Public Library.

BALLOU'S PICTORIAL DRAWING-ROOM COMPANION.

HORSELESS AGE.

The Landauer Collection in the New York Historical Society.

THOMAS NAST'S CHRISTMAS DRAWINGS OF THE HUMAN RACE. Harper and Bros. 1890.

The material in the section devoted to Alphabets and Decorative Initials was taken from the following books:

DECORATIVE INITIAL LETTERS, collected and arranged by A. F. Johnson:

Plates 3, 4, 6 to 8, 10 to 30, 52 to 54 (all inclusive)

SCHRIFTEN ATLAS, a collection made by Ludwig Petzendorfer, 1889:

Plates 32 to 35, 38 to 40, 44 to 48 (all inclusive)

EARLY WOODCUT INITIALS, selected and annotated by Oscar Jennings, M.D., in 1908:

Plates 5 and 9

SPECIMENS OF ELECTROTYPES, A. Zeese & Co., 1891:

Plates 31, 49 to 51 (inclusive)

PRANG'S STANDARD ALPHABETS, L. Prang & Co., 1878:

Plate 41

COPLEY'S PLAIN AND ORNAMENTAL STANDARD ALPHABETS, drawn and arranged by Frederick S. Copley, 1870:

Plates 36 and 37

OEUVRES DE JEAN MIDOLLE, published by Emile Simon Fils, Strasbourg, 1834-1835:

Plates 42 and 43

The following check-list from the catalogue files of the Typographic Library of Columbia University, New York, represents the most complete collection of specimen books in America. The volumes were gathered by the late Henry Lewis Bullen, acting as curator and collector for the American Type Founders Company.

ALBANY TYPE FOUNDRY, R. Starr & Co., 1826.

BALTIMORE TYPE FOUNDRY, (Fielding Lucas, Jr., agent) 1832.
" " " F. Lucas, 1851.
" " " Lucas Brothers, 1854.
" " " H. L. Pelouze & Son, 1879.

BINNEY & RONALDSON, Philadelphia, 1809.
" " " 1812.

JAMES RONALDSON, Philadelphia, 1816
" " " 1822.

BOSTON TYPE FOUNDRY, 1820.
" " " 1825.
" " " 1826, (John Rogers, agent)
" " " 1828.
" " " 1832.
" " " 1837.
" " " 1845.
" " " John K. Rogers&Co., 1853.
" " " " " " 1856.
" " " " " " 1857.
" " " " " " 1860.
" " " " " " 1864.
" " " " " " 1867.
" " " " " " 1869.
" " " " " " 1871.

BOSTON TYPE FOUNDRY, John K. Rogers&Co., 1874.
" " " " " " c. 1875.
" " " " " " 1878.
" " " " " " 1880.
" " " " " " 1883.

BRUCE, DAVID & GEORGE, New York, 1815.
" " " " " 1815-16.
" " " " " 1818.

CHANDLER, A., New York, 1822.

CINCINNATI TYPE FOUNDRY, O. & H. Wells, 1827.
" " " " " 1834.
" " " (Horace Wells, agent) 1844.
" " " (L. T. Wells, agent) 1851.
" " " " " 1852.
" " " " " c. 1853.
" " " " " 1856.

CONNER & COOKE, New York, 1834.
" " " " 1836.
" " " " 1837.
" " (Supplement to the 1836 book)

JAMES CONNER & SON, New York, 1841.
" " " " " 1850.
" " " " " 1852.
" " " " " before 1855.
" " " " " 1855.
" " " " " 1859.
" " " " " 1860.

JAMES CONNER'S SONS, New York, 1870.
" " " " " 1876.
" " " " " 1885.
" " " " " 1888.
" " " " " 1891.

DICKENSON TYPE FOUNDRY, (Samuel N. Dickenson) Boston, 1842.
" " " (Samuel N. Dickenson) Boston, 1847.
" " " (Phelps and Dalton) Boston, 1855.

FRANKLIN TYPE FOUNDRY, Allison, Smith & Johnson, Cincinnati, 1871.
" " " " 1873.

FRANKLIN LETTER-FOUNDRY, A. W. Kinsley & Company, Albany, 1829.

HAGAR, WILLIAM & CO., New York, 1826.
" " " " " 1831.
" " " " " 1841.
" " " " " 1850
" " " " " 1854.
" " " " " 1858.
" " " " " 1860.
" " " " " 1873.
" " " " " 1886.

JOHNSON & SMITH, Phila., 1834.
(Successors to Binney and Ronaldson
" " " 1841.
" " " 1843.

LAWRENCE JOHNSON, Philadelphia, 1844
" " " c. 1845.

LAWRENCE JOHNSON & CO., Phila., 1847.
" " " " 1849.
" " " " before 1853.
" " " " 1853.
" " " " 1856.
" " " " 1857.
" " " " 1859.
" " " " 1865.

MAC KELLAR, SMITHS & JORDAN, Phila., 1868.
" " " " 1869.
" " " " 1871.
" " " " 1873.
" " " " 1876.
" " " " 1877.
" " " " 1878.
" " " " 1881.
" " " " 1882.
" " " " 1884.
" " " " 1885.
" " " " 1886.
" " " " 1887.
" " " " 1888.
" " " " 1889.
" " " " 1890.
" " " " 1892.
" " " " 1894.
MAC KELLAR, SMITHS & JORDAN, Phila., 1895.
" " " " 1897.

LOTHIAN, GEORGE B., New York, 1841.

LYMAN, NATHAN & COMPANY, Buffalo, 1841.
" " " " 1853.

NEW ENGLAND TYPE FOUNDRY, Henry Willis, Boston, 1834.
" " " " George and J. Curtis, Boston, 1838.
" " " " 1841.

OHIO TYPE FOUNDRY, Guilford & Jones, Cincinnati, 1851.

PELOUZE, LEWIS, Philadelphia, 1849.

PELOUZE, LEWIS & SON, Philadelphia, 1856.

REICH, STARR & COMPANY, Philadelphia, 1818.

ROBB & ECKLIN, Philadelphia, 1836.

ALEXANDER ROBB, Philadelphia, 1844.

STARR & LITTLE, Albany, 1828.

WHITE, ELIHU, New York, 1812.
" " " " 1817.
" " " " 1821.
" " " " 1826.
" " " " 1829.